"Building on the work of philosopher C[harles Taylor,] Noble deftly describes unique modern [challenges to belief in the] Triune God and calls fellow Christians to [disrupt. Noble's] teaching gives me hope for the possibility of enfleshed Christian witness in an age that is prone to mostly shrug at ultimate questions. It will also leave more than a few of us disrupted ourselves."

Katelyn Beaty, author of *A Woman's Place*, editor-at-large at *Christianity Today*

"In our current cultural moment where self is at the center, distraction is the norm, and faith is anything you want it to be, fresh formation and evangelistic strategies are sorely needed.... For although the world has changed, the human need has remained the same—for grace *and* truth, for love *and* law, for a culture of kindness *and* a call to repent, for provision of comfort *and* prophetic disruption. In *Disruptive Witness*, Alan does a terrific job of painting a picture of what this can look like for us. I highly recommend his work to you."

Scott Sauls, senior pastor of Christ Presbyterian Church in Nashville, Tennessee, author of *Jesus Outside the Lines*

"Helpfully situating the peculiar travails and challenges to belief and fidelity in the contemporary moment, Alan Noble invites us to practice a life in Christ deeper than the fragile faith-as-preference model, which our distracted, secular age constrains us to adopt. Instead, he calls us, as both individuals and as the church, to thoughtfully contemplate our walk and our witness to Christ, so that we might not be heedlessly swept away in the patterns of thought and practice of this age. It's an appeal worth attending, not only for its clarity and urgency, but because it is one I've seen Alan embody for years in his own faithfully disruptive life and witness."

Derek Rishmawy, PhD student at Trinity Evangelical Divinity School, columnist for *Christianity Today*

"In an age of distraction and the 'buffered self,' perhaps this is more a time for preparing the soil than for reaping. In any case, Alan Noble displays the disruptive resources of Christ's kingdom that are at hand. I will be recommending this book far and wide!"

Michael Horton, professor of theology and apologetics at Westminster Seminary California, cohost on *White Horse Inn*

"The title of the book, *Disruptive Witness: Speaking Truth in a Distracted Age*, is its thesis and prescription. How do you understand, and then speak into our distracted and secular age? Noble says with disruptive witness. Following in the path of Schaeffer, Myers, Wells, Guinness, Sire, Smith, and others, Noble offers keen analysis of the situation we are living in and helpful reflection on how both to resist and engage it."

Ligon Duncan, chancellor and CEO at Reformed Theological Seminary, John E. Richards Professor of Systematic and Historical Theology

"Alan Noble is both a careful, clearheaded thinker, and a passionate advocate for truth in a post-truth culture. I can think of few people who would serve as better guides for navigating the complex and frustrating culture we inhabit. This book is a must-read for those hoping that the church can maintain a bold and faithful witness in the days to come."

Mike Cosper, author of *Recapturing the Wonder* and *Faith Among the Faithless*

"While reading *Disruptive Witness* I got more than a little tired of Alan Noble reading my mind, diagnosing my issues, and jabbing at the nerves of my heart. Page after page he hit on issues of thought, habit, perspective, or lifestyle with which I struggle and in which I fail to be a proper witness for Jesus. Of course what I was really tired of was my own distracted, thin faith. And those are the very things this book helps. Noble clearly and gently diagnoses the problems first and then he offers robust solutions. *Disruptive Witness* is incisive, substantial, and encouraging for tired, frustrated believers looking for direction."

Barnabas Piper, author and podcaster

"I puzzle a lot about how to bring the claims of the gospel to bear on a changing culture that regularly bewilders me. Now I find out in this book that Alan Noble checks his Twitter account before he gets out of bed in the morning, and he watches Netflix while doing the dishes. He also knows a lot about vampirism. And then he reflects on all of this in the light of what he has read by Charles Taylor, John Calvin, Jamie Smith, and Blaise Pascal. Wow! IMHO this book is awesome."

Richard J. Mouw, president emeritus, professor of faith and public life at Fuller Theological Seminary

DISRUPTIVE WITNESS

SPEAKING TRUTH IN

A DISTRACTED AGE

ALAN NOBLE

IVP Books

An imprint of InterVarsity Press
Downers Grove, Illinois

InterVarsity Press
P.O. Box 1400, Downers Grove, IL 60515-1426
ivpress.com
email@ivpress.com

InterVarsity Press® is the book-publishing division of InterVarsity Christian Fellowship/USA®, a movement of
students and faculty active on campus at hundreds of universities, colleges, and schools of nursing in the United
States of America, and a member movement of the International Fellowship of Evangelical Students. For
information about local and regional activities, visit intervarsity.org.

Scripture quotations, unless otherwise noted, are from The Holy Bible, English Standard Version, copyright © 2001
by Crossway Bibles, a division of Good News Publishers. Used by permission. All rights reserved.

While any stories in this book are true, some names and identifying information may have been changed to protect
the privacy of individuals.

Published in association with the literary agent Don Gates of The Gates Group, www.the-gates-group.com.

Cover design and image composite: David Fassett
Interior design: Daniel van Loon
Images: abstract background: © serkorkin / iStock / Getty Images Plus
         Jesus Christ: © kadmy / iStock / Getty Images Plus

ISBN 978-0-8308-4483-8 (print)
ISBN 978-0-8308-8109-3 (digital)

Printed in the United States of America ∞

InterVarsity Press is committed to ecological stewardship and to the conservation of natural resources in all our
operations. This book was printed using sustainably sourced paper.

Library of Congress Cataloging-in-Publication Data

Names: Noble, Alan, 1981- author.
Title: Disruptive witness : speaking truth in a distracted age / Alan Noble.
Description: Downers Grove : InterVarsity Press, 2018. | Includes
   bibliographical references.
Identifiers: LCCN 2018012243 (print) | LCCN 2018020398 (ebook) | ISBN
   9780830881093 (eBook) | ISBN 9780830844838 (pbk. : alk. paper)
Subjects: LCSH: Christianity and culture. | Witness bearing (Christianity)
Classification: LCC BR115.C8 (ebook) | LCC BR115.C8 N625 2018 (print) | DDC
   261—dc23
LC record available at https://lccn.loc.gov/2018012243

P   24   23   22   21   20   19   18   17   16   15   14   13   12   11   10   9   8   7   6   5   4   3
Y   37   36   35   34   33   32   31   30   29   28   27   26   25   24   23   22   21   20   19   18

For my mother, Brenda,

who taught me to read, to learn, and to think.

CONTENTS

INTRODUCTION

What if the vast majority of our conversations about Christianity are not really about our faith at all? What if we are so accustomed to thinking about our beliefs in terms of personal preferences, like sports teams or our favorite brands, that when we try to share the gospel with someone, neither of us are actually thinking about the existence and lordship of a loving God who died on the cross for our sins? Even if, by some chance, one of us does manage to envision the idea of a transcendent God, it is only for a moment, because we just got a text message from our spouse about what to have for dinner tonight. Then we check Twitter, and then we read an article, and then—it's gone.

What if our most passionate and articulate conversations about the gospel with our unbelieving neighbors are actually orchestrated social games, which both sides leave without having wagered anything? We walk away satisfied that we scored some points, and then unlock our phones and forget it ever happened. We may genuinely believe we "shared the gospel," but all we did was participate in a kind of rhetorical dance that didn't haunt or unsettle our neighbor at all. Our neighbor knows there are other beliefs out there, other religions and philosophies to choose from. And besides, there are so many more interesting and distracting things for them to do than to reflect on the gospel. So they leave the conversation untouched by our words, and we leave feeling vaguely pleased with ourselves.

The work of conviction and calling is the Holy Spirit's, but different times and cultures present different barriers to hearing and comprehending the good news. Identifying, understanding, and overcoming these barriers with God's grace and wisdom has always been the Christian's holy task, whether our neighbors are devout Jews, Greeks worshiping an unknown god, or contemporary Americans. And I believe the convergence of two major trends in our own time calls for a new assessment of the barriers to faith. This assessment involves much more than how to overcome objections to faith, but also the extent to which the church in America has accommodated ideas and practices that make it difficult for us to bear witness.

These two major trends are (1) the practice of continuous engagement in immediately gratifying activities that resist reflection and meditation, and (2) the growth of secularism, defined as a state in which theism is seen as one of many viable choices for human fullness and satisfaction, and in which the transcendent feels less and less plausible. One result of these trends is that, as evangelicals, when we speak of Christianity we cannot assume that our hearers understand the faith as anything other than another personal preference in an ocean of cultural preferences. In such a world, the work of witnessing and defending the faith must involve rethinking how we communicate.

The electronic buzz of the twenty-first century combined with the proliferation of personal stories of meaning (what I call "micronarratives of justification," as opposed to "metanarratives") has helped create what we may call *distracted, buffered selves*. The Canadian philosopher Charles Taylor coined the term *buffered self* to refer to the way modern people imagine themselves to be insulated from forces outside their rational mind, particularly supernatural or transcendent forces.[1] The buffered self is a particular result of living in the closed, physical universe (Taylor calls it the "immanent frame"), in which everything has a natural explanation. Nearly all contemporary Western people, including Christians, use this frame to interpret the world.

Our pervasive culture of technological distraction dramatically exacerbates the effects of the buffered self, which in turn feeds the demand for technology of distraction. It is not a coincidence that these two forces have arisen at this point in history. The rise of secularism has inspired a view of technology and fullness rooted thoroughly in this life and established and chosen inwardly, which I believe has helped to justify the creation and adoption of technologies that are not directed toward human flourishing but instead help us project our identity and remain distracted. Outside of a culture of virtue grounded in an external source, science, technology, and the market have been driven to produce a society that prioritizes the sovereign individual.

The modern person experiences a buffer between themselves and the world out there—including transcendent ideas and truths. The constant distraction of our culture shields us from the kind of deep, honest reflection needed to ask why we exist and what is true.

The value of individual choice and the multiplication of micro-narratives shield us from committing to a consistent and coherent worldview. This allows the modern person to debate religion and politics freely, without any anxiety about what is at stake—because very little *is* at stake. Between the buzz of our lives and the fluidity of our narratives, there's no reason any truth should ever threaten our understanding of the world or ourselves. Perhaps as a result, Christianity and atheism have never been as debated as they have in the last decade. But because of our buffered selves, what is at stake in such debates is a sense of superiority or social accolades, not whether we must sell everything we have, give to the poor, and follow Jesus.

Speaking to the kind of culture I've described requires a different kind of rhetoric than what we may be accustomed to. Often, direct conversations about God, sin, and salvation can be easily co-opted into one of the hearer's narratives without any real obligation on them. I witnessed a moving example of this phenomenon when I worked as an English tutor at a camp for high school felons. Most of the felons came from communities defined by gang culture. Their uncles and fathers and brothers were all in the gang, and so it was natural for them to join that lifestyle too. If given the freedom, the boys loved swapping stories of violence, drug and alcohol abuse, or sex. What fascinated me was that a good number of them also believed in God and were open to hearing about the gospel. They would speak contritely about their sins and their desire to change, but ultimately most of them would conclude that they were stuck. They knew they were sinners. They knew their lifestyle would kill them and make their mothers cry and that God would condemn them, but it was too late to change, they would insist.

It took me a few months to realize that for many of these youths, Christ dying on the cross for their sins and rising again was not a reality. It was just another character or plot point in the drama of their lives. The narrative of a violent criminal who knows his sin and yet can never fully leave that lifestyle is much more tragic and moving than the story of a man who is unquestionably reprobate. There was an element of Greek tragedy to their view of God. They were tragically caught in a life of defiance against God. When I spoke to them about the saving power of Christ, I conceived of it as a reality with its roots in historical past, its implications for the present, and its hope for the future. But they saw it as a foil in their own, more immediate and satisfying drama of life. And maybe the way I presented the gospel made it hard for them to imagine Christ as real. In a culture where the gospel can be so easily co-opted into individual narratives without any honest spiritual response by a person, how can we witness to the truth of the gospel and defend it so that it goes beyond the hearer's buffer?

The first and most important answer to any question about effective witness and apologetics is reliance on the Holy Spirit. God is the one who works his will, and he will call people to himself. But we are still obligated to plant the seed; moreover we are obligated to plant it *well*. So, the question for modern evangelicals in America is, How can we plant the seed of the gospel deeply into the soil so it might take root?

We need to plow. One of Christ's most well-known parables is the parable of the sower in Matthew 13:3-9, in which Jesus describes how people receive the gospel. Some seeds fall on a path and are eaten by birds—representing those who do not understand the Word. Some fall on rocky ground and soon wither—representing those who receive the Word but abandon it when suffering comes. Some fall among thorns and are choked—representing the deadly cares of this world. Finally, some fall on good soil and produce a hundredfold—representing those who hear and understand the Word. If you have spent any length of time in the church, this parable is very familiar to you, so familiar, perhaps, as to become trivial. But have you ever thought about this good soil? How did it become good?

Imagine the sower going down a path to his field to sow the season's crops. As he reaches the edge of the field, he begins spreading the seeds, and because he has just stepped off the path, some of those seeds unintentionally fall on it. But what is the field itself like? Are we to think that our sower walked to some vacant field and began casting seeds, willy-nilly, indifferent to the quality of the soil? No good farmer would plant this way. Before the action of Christ's parable begins, the sower has been to this field. He has worked it, maybe for days, plowing the ground, pulling weeds, moving rocks. The sower can't remove every rock and weed; some seeds will inevitably wither or be choked. And no sower can guaranty the yield of the crop, but by cultivating the ground, the sower can help the seed take root.

Unlike the gentle act of sowing seeds, a plow's work is violent, disruptive, and exhausting. It unsettles the ground. It softens by tearing up. When a field has been plowed it no longer appears the same. The hard surface has been broken to reveal the vulnerable but fertile womb of the earth. It is much easier to simply cast the seeds and hope for a harvest, but a good farmer knows that the ground needs cultivation. This is the work of witnessing in the twenty-first century. We need to focus on what takes place just before the parable of the sower begins. Our task is to communicate our faith and the truths of our world in such a way as to disrupt our buffered and distracted culture.

THE GROUND AHEAD

To understand the contemporary challenge of bearing witness to the truth of the gospel of Jesus Christ, we need to consider our way of life in this distracted age, and what effect it has on our ability to reflect, contemplate, and respond to conviction. With the help of Charles Taylor and others, we will explore what it means to live in a *secular age* and how this compounds the effects of distraction to create a deep and largely unacknowledged barrier to belief for most people. There are no easy answers to the problems created by our contemporary condition, but by changing our personal habits, recovering church practices that convey God's holiness, and rethinking how we participate in culture, we can offer a disruptive witness that will help people to see the world anew, as created by a living and sustaining God.

The work of the gospel is always the work of the Holy Spirit, but we are called to use language that lays the truth of the gospel bare. Paul says in 2 Corinthians 4:3, "If our gospel is veiled, it is veiled to those who are perishing." My admonition in this book is to understand how our culture processes beliefs, so we might better fulfill our duty to love our neighbor and glorify God.

PART ONE

A DISTRACTED, SECULAR AGE

1

THE BARRIER OF ENDLESS DISTRACTION

The person I'm most uncomfortable being alone with is myself. And that's okay, because I've become very good at avoiding myself. For example, if I get stuck alone on an elevator, and I start to feel that anxiety, the dread of having to examine my life—even for a minute—I just take out my phone, and poof! it's gone. Or if I sense that I need to have a heart-to-heart talk with myself about sin or doubt or fear, all of a sudden I remember that it's my night to do the dishes—and I can't do the dishes without listening to a podcast.

Self-avoidance is probably my most advanced skill set. I've developed it over the years in response to the burden of being alone, which can bring up so many unsettling truths. Of course, I have plenty of help from the rest of society. I'm always being encouraged to read something, to do something, to watch something, or to buy something new. It's an unspoken but mutually agreed upon truth for modern people that being alone with our thoughts is disturbing.

A friend once described a similar feeling of existential dread to me. He said it would hit him only when he woke up in the morning. Sometimes he'd feel like killing himself. It wasn't something he shared with friends. But he'd get this sick feeling—like there's no point to any of it—every morning. He said he needed something more to get him up in the morning. My friend could stave off this sense of hopelessness all day, except for those few moments right after he woke up. Lying in bed, he could feel the pressure of being alive constrict his breath. But once he got moving, drank his coffee, watched the news, and went to work, he was okay. He got swept up into the movement of the day, as most of us do.

A DISTRACTED AND DISENCHANTED DAY IN THE LIFE

The beauty of using my iPhone as my alarm clock is that when I reach over to turn it off I'm only a few more taps away from the rest of the world. Before I'm even fully awake I've checked my Twitter and Facebook notifications and my email and returned to Twitter to check my feed for breaking news. Before I've said "good morning" to my wife and children, I've entered a contentious argument on Twitter about Islamic terrorism and shared a video of Russell Westbrook dunking in the previous night's NBA game.

While making my coffee and breakfast I begin working through social media conversations that require more detailed responses so that by the time I sit down to eat, I can set down my phone too. Years ago I would use my early morning grouchiness as an excuse to play on my computer rather than talk with my wife and kids, but now our family tries to stay faithful to a strict no-phones-at-the-table policy. We have drawn important boundaries for the encroachment of technology into our lives to preserve our family and attention spans, but that does not mean we've managed to save time for reflection. Instead, I tend to use this time to go over what I have to teach in my first class, or my wife and I make a list of goals for the day. It is a time of rest from screens and technology, but not from preoccupation.

As I drive the kids to school, we listen and sing along to "Reflektor" by Arcade Fire. On my walk back to the car after dropping them off, I check my email and make a few more comments in the Twitter debate I began before breakfast. In the car again, I listen to an NBA fan podcast; it relaxes me a bit as the anxiety of the coming work day continues to creep up on me.

Sufficient to the workday are the anxieties and frustrations thereof. And so, when I need a coffee or bathroom break, I'll use my phone to skim an article or like a few posts. The distraction is a much-needed relief from the stress of work, but it also *is* a distraction. I still can't hear myself think. And most of the time I really don't want to. When I feel some guilt about spending so much time being unfocused, I tell myself it's for my own good. I deserve this break. I need this break. But there's no break from distraction.

While at work, I try not to think about social media and the news, but I really don't need additional distractions to keep my mind busy. The modern work environment is just as frenetic and unfocused as our leisure time. A constant stream of emails breaks my focus and shifts my train of thought between multiple projects. To do any seriously challenging task, I often have to get up and take a walk to absorb myself in the problem without the immediacy of technology to throw me off.

Back at home, I'm tasked with watching the kids. They are old enough to play on their own, so I find myself standing around, waiting for one of them to tattle or get hurt or need water for the fifth time. If I planned ahead, I might read a book, but usually I use the time to check Twitter and Facebook or read a short online article. But it's not always technology that distracts me; sometimes, while the kids are briefly playing well together, I'll do some housecleaning or pay bills. Whatever the method, I'm always leaning forward to the next job, the next comment, the next goal.

I watch Netflix while I wash dishes. I follow NBA scores while I grade. I panic for a moment when I begin to go upstairs to get something. I turn around and find my phone to keep me company during the two-minute trip. When it's late enough, I collapse, reading a book or playing an iOS game. I'm never alone and it's never quiet.

As a Christian, the spiritual disciplines of reading the Bible and praying offer me a chance to reflect, but it's too easy to turn these times into to-do list chores as well.[1] Using my Bible app, I get caught up in the Greek meaning of a word and the contextual notes and never really meditate on the Word itself. It is an exercise, not an encounter with the sacred, divine Word of God. A moleskin prayer journal might help me remember God's faithfulness, but it also might mediate my prayer time through a self-conscious pride in being devout. There's no space in our modern lives that can't be filled up with entertainment, socializing, recording, or commentary.

This has always been the human condition. The world has always moved without us and before us and after us, and we quickly learn how to swim with the current. We make sense of our swimming by observing our fellow swimmers and hearing their stories. We conceive of these narratives based on the stories we've heard elsewhere: from our communities, the media, advertisements, or traditions.

But for the twenty-first-century person in an affluent country like the United States, the momentum of life that so often discourages us from stopping to take our bearings is magnified dramatically by the constant hum of portable electronic entertainment, personalized for our interests and desires and delivered over high-speed wireless internet. It's not just that this technology allows us to stay "plugged in" all the time, it's that it gives us the sense that we are tapped into something greater than ourselves. The narratives of meaning that have always filled our lives with justification and wonder are multiplied endlessly and immediately for us in songs, TV shows, online communities, games, and the news.

This is the electronic buzz of the twenty-first century. And it is suffocating.

THE MINDFULNESS SOLUTION

Maybe your typical day doesn't resemble the perpetually distracted and frantic experience I've just described. But there's a good chance you suffer from the electronic buzz of the twenty-first century all the same, even if to a smaller extent. Aside from studies and polls where people have self-identified as busier than ever before, one sign that this is a common experience is the sudden popularity of mindfulness techniques. There are mindfulness gurus, seminars, books, and counseling methods. In that ever-profitable marketing space where self-help, spirituality, and psychology meet, mindfulness dominates. This technique addresses a common problem for many: a sense of frenetic emptiness.

Americans have long been fascinated with Eastern meditation, but its recent manifestation as "mindfulness" is distinct from earlier interest in transcendental meditation. Whereas the latter necessarily included a deep desire for spiritual growth, the former is more concerned with efficiency and being well balanced. Mindfulness is religion for lifehackers, we might say. The central principle to mindfulness is focusing on the immediacy of the present and our experience of being in this moment. To a great extent, our society has worked to keep us from this reality. We are oriented toward the future and what still needs to be done, and when we focus on the now or the past, we do so in a disengaged way. For example, we prefer to focus on which Instagram filter looks best than on enjoying the scene we've just photographed. This is a basic feature of modern life, which sociologist Thomas de Zengotita refers to as "mediated" living.[2]

In his book *Mediated: How the Media Shapes Your World and the Way You Live in It*, de Zengotita argues that we experience our world with a hyperawareness of representation. So, for example, when we go for a walk in the woods alone, we are never merely going for a walk in the woods alone; our experience of nature is filtered through the Instagram pictures we take and our awareness of how our friends will experience those pictures, and how they will think about us in light of those pictures.[3] Or we might mediate the walk through an outdoors hipster aesthetic that we've pieced together from indie folk band album covers. Or we might mediate the walk through an awareness of global warming and its effects on the environment. However we conceive of the walk, it is never *simply* a walk in the woods. Of course, to some extent, this has always been our human experience; we've always experienced life as an interconnected web. But with the tremendous growth of technology and the media, of life as public performance, our ability to resist mediation has declined. In our world, we have to fight harder to experience the present shorn of stultifying mediation. And that fight is for *mindfulness*.

In addition to the problem of overwhelming mediation, mindfulness seeks to silence the voices and distractions in our lives. Typically, mindfulness training involves sitting silently for a period of time or for formal meditation. There is a tremendous focus on breathing and its ability to center us. And through these practices, we hope to learn to be present in the world and aware of our existence.

While once primarily popular among those in Silicon Valley, the mindfulness movement has now grown into a major method of psychological treatment and a multimillion-dollar industry. An article in the *Telegraph* dubbed it the saddest trend of 2015.[4] And perhaps there is something sad about devoting such time and money in order to hear ourselves think once in awhile. But this trend is not a Luddite reaction to technology. The mindfulness movement is not an antitechnology movement but an

17

attempt to find healthier ways to live with the technology we can't seem to live without.

Although I think there's much to be said for this strategy of addressing our perpetually distracted and mediated lives, my concern in this book is with how the church can speak more prophetically in such a world. Because whether modern technology is on the whole harming society, and whether mindfulness practices will have any significant mitigating effect on this harm, for the vast majority of Americans, this overly integrated and frantic world is the culture we live in. Mindfulness training requires more time and money than most of us can afford.

In this rise of the mindfulness industry, we can see a tension between technological changes and our deep desire for a more immediate and integrated world. No question, these practices are addressing a serious problem in society, but they are also a symptom of a society driven by technological innovation, where how we *ought* to live follows far behind how we *can* live. And we have every reason to believe that technology will continue to drive our world.

TECHNOLOGICAL CHANGES

Modern media technology focuses largely on two goals: capturing our attention and gathering our data. While the latter has troubling implications for our privacy, the former has a direct effect on our ability to encounter and contemplate the holy.

Innumerable gadgets, websites, channels, streaming services, songs, films, and biometric wristbands vie for our attention. Without our attention, their existence is unjustified. So, each piece of technology we own does what it can to make us pay attention to it, like an overly eager child tugging on our sleeve, begging, "Look what I can do, Dad!" It is not just that every spare moment is fought for; our technology covets every glance. Flashing lights, vibrations, bells ringing, little red dots, email alerts, notifications, pop-up windows, commercials, news tickers, browser tabs—everything is designed to capture our attention.

And there is good reason to believe that technology will only continue to progress in this direction. Unless you are a mindfulness guru, you don't have much incentive to encourage your customers to slow down, declutter, and unplug. The momentum in the technology industries is toward more opportunities for engagement and entertainment. For example, self-driving cars will prevent millions of deaths and reduce traffic, but they will also enable us to use commute time to surf the web—safely.

A reactionary stance argues that these changes are inherently harmful to the human mind and culture, and the uncritical embrace of these technologies has led to a widespread decline in human flourishing. This is an argument that discerning Christians would do well to consider. It is important for us as Christians and as consumers to question the unintended consequences of changes in technology. But we should not naively believe that we can suddenly reverse the flow of innovation. Barring a catastrophic event or a dramatic shift in the structure and goals of modern technology, we can expect that for the foreseeable future our society will be in part defined by technology designed to continually distract us. Wise Christians will discern how to appropriately use new media and technology, not withdraw and rail against it.

To live well in a modern world requires constant reassessment of how our society and technology are shaping us. We should be open to taking drastic steps to reject practices and habits that we believe are destructive or evil. But the vast majority of innovations will not be so clear-cut, and we will have to weigh benefits, purposes, and damaging effects individually and in community.[5] But as with mindfulness training, whatever efforts we personally take to resist getting sucked into the electronic buzz of the twenty-first century, the vast majority of our neighbors will be caught in the stream.

If we assume that for the most part society will continue down the path of adopting invasive and distracting technologies, the question facing Christians becomes not only how can we resist these changes but also how can we speak the truth in a culture where this is the norm? But before we may answer this, we must consider how truth is interpreted in this kind of world. What effect does this technology have on our minds? And how does that affect our ability to interpret spiritual truths, to conceive of a God who transcends our material world?

MENTALLY SPENT

Living a distracted lifestyle does more than waste our time, it forms our minds, often in ways that are harmful for deep, sustained thought—the kind of thought so important to religious discourse. Armed with these concerns, neurologists have been looking closely at the effects of distraction and constant connection to the internet. The American cognitive scientist Daniel J. Levitin has surveyed these findings in *The Organized Mind*.

Levitin explains that multitasking, which we are increasingly pressured to do by our technology and society, has serious physiological effects on our brains.

Multitasking has been found to increase the production of the stress hormone cortisol as well as the fight-or-flight hormone adrenaline, which can overstimulate your brain and cause mental fog or scrambled thinking. Multitasking creates a dopamine-addiction feedback loop, effectively rewarding the brain for losing focus and for constantly searching for external stimulation. To make matters worse, the prefrontal cortex has a novelty bias, meaning that its attention can be easily hijacked by something new—the proverbial shiny objects we use to entice infants, puppies, and kittens. The irony here for those of us who are trying to focus amid competing activities is clear: the very brain region we need to rely on for staying on task is easily distracted. We answer the phone, look up something on the internet, check our email, send an SMS, and each of these things tweaks the novelty-seeking, reward-seeking centers of the brain, causing a burst of endogenous opioids (no wonder it feels so good!), all to the detriment of our staying on task.[6]

We are addicted to novelty, and as with most addictions, it takes a toll on our bodies: we become mentally fatigued, "scrambled," as Levitin describes it. In this way, the modern mind is often not prepared to engage in dialogue about personally challenging ideas, particularly ones with deep implications. The fatigued mind would rather categorize a conversation about God as another superficial distraction, requiring little cognitive attention, than a serious conversation that ought to cost us, at least cognitively.

The shape of our engagement with ideas forms how we interpret and categorize these ideas. Both the kind of technology we use and the way we use it can lead us to mislabel information. Levitin notes that multitasking is one cause of improperly categorizing information.

> Russ Poldrack, a neuroscientist at Stanford, found that learning information while multitasking causes the new information to go to the wrong part of the brain. If students study and watch TV at the same time, for example, the information from their schoolwork goes into the striatum, a region specialized for storing new procedures and skills, not facts and ideas. Without the distraction of TV, the information goes into the hippocampus, where it is organized and categorized in a variety of ways, making it easier to retrieve.[7]

Presumably this kind confusion happens regularly for most people, since so much of our engagement with Christianity takes place in a multitasking space. You might see a billboard promoting biblical morality while driving and listening to an audiobook. Or your grandmother shares a YouTube clip of her pastor's sermon on Facebook, which you watch while you are texting a friend. You may even find yourself multitasking while reading this book, but probably not, because the form of a book works against a distracted mind. Aside from endnotes, a book is a fairly linear form. It does not invite you to jump around cognitively, but to follow a carefully crafted argument, sentence by sentence, paragraph by paragraph, page by page. But of course, much of modern technology isn't this way. If you are reading this on a digital device, your brain is quite aware of how easy it would be to shift over to your email or text messages. And if you have your notifications turned on, you may be fighting a losing battle. An effect of your multitasking may be that the information you take in ends up in the wrong place, a kind of seed falling on rocky cognitive soil.

In addition, Levitin notes that there has been a general flattening of methods of communication. Most of our communication has shifted toward one or two methods: email and texting.

> Emails are used for all of life's messages. We compulsively check our email in part because we don't know whether the next message will be for leisure/amusement, an overdue bill, a "to do," a query . . . something you can do now, later, something life-changing, something irrelevant.
>
> This uncertainty wreaks havoc with our rapid perceptual categorization system, causes stress, and leads to decision overload. Every email requires a decision! Do I respond to it? If so, now or later? How important is it? What will be the social, economic, or job-related consequences if I don't answer, or if I don't answer right now?[8]

The space between the trivial and the crucial has shrunk. Everything is important all of the time, and you are obligated to keep up. Just as it is harder for us to sort all our correspondence when it comes in the same medium, it can be difficult for us to communicate the gospel if we primarily use mediums that are traditionally devoted to triviality.

Levitin describes how the flattening of distinctions "leads to decision overload." Multitasking forces us to make millions of tiny decisions (What song should I listen to? Should I share this article? Should I check that text message? How should I reply to this email?), and this wears us out cognitively. The result is that when it comes time for us to make important decisions, we are too exhausted and are more likely to make mistakes. Alternatively, we may avoid making a decision all together. When there are an almost infinite number of options, it is hard to choose one.

Decision overload is as much a problem for spirituality as it is for digital multitasking. A good friend of mine once explained that although he believed there is a God, he didn't know which religious account of God is true because there are so many different religions. When I asked him why he didn't try to discover the truth, he replied that it was just too overwhelming. A distracted and secular age does this to us: we are cognitively overwhelmed by the expanding horizon of possible beliefs.

Our frenetic and flattened culture is not conducive to wrestling with thick ideas, ideas with depth, complexity, and personal implications. It is a culture of immediacy, simple emotions, snap judgments, optics, and identity formation. In such a world, is it any wonder that Christians so often speak past their listeners?

I am not making an argument against the use of modern technology. People who use email and text messaging regularly are not less likely to convert to Christianity—so far as I know. Nor is conversion dependent on proper psychological conditions; the Holy Spirit's call is not constrained by such things. The point is that our past models of discussing faith have almost all assumed a listener who is active, attentive, and aware of the costs of believing—a listener who conceives of a thick world. But as we have moved to a distracted age, we can no longer make this assumption.

WHERE IS MY MIND?

A lifestyle of distraction will shape the way we interpret and respond to questions about basic beliefs—how we conceive of human worth, what transcendent hopes we have, what we believe about goodness and beauty. The distracted age has three major effects on our ability to communicate about matters of faith and ultimate meaning: (1) it is easier to ignore contradictions and flaws in our basic beliefs, (2) we are less likely to devote time to introspection, and (3) conversations about faith can be easily perceived as just another exercise in superficial identity formation.

A natural consequence of being mentally engaged all the time is, first, that it is easy for us to live with internal conflicts and contradictions with little cognitive dissonance. When confronted with a deficiency in our ethical code, it takes no real effort to ignore it. Imagine, for example, someone who believes that people who rely on government assistance are freeloaders, but then this same person cheats on her taxes in little ways. Her hypocrisy should cause her a pang of guilt, but guilt requires attention in order to grow into reflection and repentance. And the structure of our day and our bodily habits are so oriented toward the next thing that she soon finds herself onto some other concern. We are certainly still capable of reflection and meditation, but our default response to cognitive dissonance is to simply do something else. The rhythms and practices of our modern world militate against reflection. There are so many immediate incentives for going with the flow; meanwhile, the recognition that we are not living up to the moral standards we identify with is costly. It certainly requires time, but it may also require changes to our lifestyle or to our moral standards. When we think of cognitive dissonance as the problem, rather than a symptom of an incoherent belief system, there are a number of effective and less costly ways of fixing things by moving on.

So, a belief in the essential goodness of humanity can live quite comfortably alongside a racist suspicion that certain people are inherently more prone to criminality. We are not interested in sorting through the validity of our convictions. We are about the next thing.

A superficial but constant engagement with media also invites us to unreflectively adopt ethical and political positions, creating a hodgepodge worldview. From a film on the treatment of animals in amusement parks we develop a fleeting concern for animal rights. A documentary on modern farming practices makes us see shopping local and organic as a moral issue. A hashtag campaign draws our attention to the evils of human trafficking, perhaps even while we look at porn on another browser tab. *Causes* are as easy to pick up as they are to put down. Or, more accurately, we don't put causes down so much as we forget them. Putting them down would require some intentional meditation on the validity of the cause. Instead, we simply move on to something else. Humans are tremendously gifted at hypocrisy and inconsistency, but a ubiquitous, powerful stream of information and interaction driven by technology enables these gifts to flourish. And that is precisely the problem.

Second, the distracted age discourages us from spending time on rich introspection. Deep questions require deep reflection. That is not to say that a fulfilling and coherent vision of life depends on being wealthy enough to sit around contemplating existence. The Christian faith has always been accessible to people without leisure time and with little educational attainment. Reflection can take place while you are doing manual labor, making a meal, falling asleep, or walking to work. Some of my best thinking has happened while washing dishes or sweeping the floor. (This does not mean that material conditions have no negative effects on reflection and belief. It's hard to think on an empty stomach.) And in some sense, being more prosperous has allowed Americans to more effectively hide from their own thoughts. The problem occurs when antipathy toward sustained introspection and soul searching, cultivated through habitual distraction, becomes a barrier for hearing the gospel. Reflection invites us to consider the contrary commitments we have in life, but it requires time and attention—our scarcest resources.

Why does our avoidance of slow, careful introspection matter? The gospel is cognitively costly. It upsets our innate and cultivated assumptions about power and guilt and existential validation. It presses down on our values and hopes. It decenters our perception of the world. Life ceases to be our story and is revealed to be his redemptive story of glory and love. It convicts us of our sins. It reveals our disordered desires and reforms them into Christ's image. Paul urges his readers to "be transformed by the renewal of your mind" (Romans 12:2), and that renewal is the proper work of the Spirit through the gospel. The kind of work the gospel does in our lives tasks our minds with unsettling assumptions and habits.

The third challenge for evangelism is that our tendency to adopt the latest media trends often adds to the buzz instead of effectively penetrating sinners' hearts. Even evangelicals who spurn seeker-friendly church outreach and "relevant" evangelism heed Paul's example of being "all things to all people" in other ways (1 Corinthians 9:22), and in a culture of sound bites, viral videos, and hashtags, this regularly involves adopting the media-rich practices that so deeply shape our culture. But in developing our own viral images and mobile apps to reach connected readers, we risk contributing to the clutter and distraction of modern life rather than helping to lift our neighbors out of it. Even more concerning, by adopting these ephemeral cultural expressions, we may signal to our neighbors that Christianity is merely another consumer preference in the endless sea of preferences we use to define ourselves as individuals.

This point was driven home to me when I received an email promoting a Christian mobile video game. The developer wanted to give me early access to this game that they hoped would be played in churches across the nation and would lead to countless souls saved. The game play was very familiar—a matching game in the vein of massive hits like *Bejeweled* and *Candy Crush Saga*— except Christian. The logic behind the game made a certain kind of sense: millions of people play mobile games, and matching puzzle games are among the most popular kinds of games; therefore, a Christian mobile matching puzzle game could be used to share the gospel with millions.

What the marketing email did not acknowledge is the mental state people are in when they play mobile games. For many, playing a game on your phone is the ultimate modern distraction. We do it while walking, using the bathroom, or cooking. Mobile games even challenge the iconic modern distraction: TV. We need distractions from our distractions, and at the bottom of all those distractions we find mobile games. No matter how articulate the gospel voice-overs are in the game, if its function is to take us further from mindfulness, it's not going to be an effective witnessing tool.

We also see this trivializing of the Christian faith in some attempts at online evangelism. Take, for example, "Jesus Daily," the "inspirational" Facebook page with over 32 million followers, the self-proclaimed "#1 most active Facebook Faith Page in history." "Jesus Daily" is active, very active. Tapping into all of the most sensational and like-able pictures and videos and stories, "Jesus Daily" is a constant stream of inspiration in its thinnest and most vapid forms. In one image an eerily drawn Jesus stretches out his hand toward you, asking, "Will you except my gift?" On the bottom of the image a watermark reads "INVITE SOMEONE TO JESUS DAILY (R)." The line between proclaiming Christ online and trying to "go viral" is obliterated, as is the distinction between proclaiming Christ and promoting "Jesus Daily." For fans of "Jesus Daily," sharing these inspirational images may be a way of declaring their faith or witnessing to the world or signaling to friends what they believe. But to their friends the images are indistinguishable from all the other random content we quickly share and forget on social media. The gospel appears thin, superficial, and inconsequential—just another image vying for our time.

Like the producers of the Christian mobile game, the church is often tempted to look at popular communication in culture and mimic it with a Christian message. And while mimicking the methods of communication in wider culture can sometimes be valuable, it can also unintentionally signal to readers that Christianity is just like all these other ideas. Rather than the disruptive force of revelation that the gospel truly is, our witness makes it just another personal preference, like our favorite bands, pet peeves, political parties, and shopping organic. The challenge for Christians in our time is to speak of the gospel in a way that unsettles listeners, that conveys the transcendence of God, that provokes contemplation and reflection, and that reveals the stark givenness of reality.

Evangelism is not only about creating space for contemplation, as if our faith was merely an act of intellectual assent. But, taking the model offered by James K. A. Smith in *Desiring the Kingdom*, I contend that our cultural practices are also a major part of how we come to believe.[9] The habits we adopt form our desires, which drive our beliefs. When those habits form desires for immediacy, superficiality, continual engagement, and instant gratification, we should expect our beliefs to reflect these desires. The content of our beliefs will be formed by our habits, but so will the nature of our beliefs. Specifically, a distracted age presents beliefs as fragile, fragmented, internal, changing, individual preferences. This conception of belief is supported by the effects of our secular age, and together these trends create a barrier to belief in the transcendent, exclusive gospel of Jesus Christ.

2

THE BARRIER OF THE BUFFERED SELF

'm a male witch, not a warlock," my coworker in the Sears electronics department informed me. His teeth were dark brown and jagged from smoking and drinking coffee and, I suppose, not brushing his teeth, which I suspected had something to do with being a witch, although I don't know what. Are there dental hygiene risks to being a witch?

He was very good at sales. Big screen TVs were about the only thing anyone made a decent commission on in our department. I think I sold two the entire six months I worked there. My coworker probably sold one every week or two. I started to wonder whether he was using spells to persuade customers. He would come to work wearing black pants, a black dress shirt, and a black trench coat. On a chain around his neck he wore a chrome skull with cheap black stones for eyes. His hair was slicked back, Malfoy style. His most notable affectation was his cane. It was black with a large silver knob at the top and a silver tip on the bottom. There was no medical reason for the cane; it was just part of the show.

I used to wonder if he really thought he was a witch. How deep did this obsession go? So, when he asked me for a ride home from work one night, I didn't mind going out of my way. I figured that once I got him alone, away from an audience of coworkers and customers, he would put down his guard, stop playing the part, and just be himself. But I was disappointed—he never broke character. It was a long drive home.

I left that job as soon as I could, but I ran into my old coworker a few months later. He had been promoted to the assistant store manager, second only to the store manager. He seemed happy and was certainly proud of what he had accomplished, moving from the sales floor all the way to the penultimate position. But he was still playing the part, dressed in the same gothic outfit, still overdramatically swinging the same cane, and grinning with those same dingy teeth. And it made some sense to see him be so successful in sales. There was a cutthroat quality to our work that fit his persona well. While working with him, I remember thinking, *Does anyone else notice that he's a witch? Or is this just me? Do y'all not see this?* It felt like it should be an issue, like it ought to disrupt our work environment and cost him sales, but it didn't. Not at all. If anything, this persona aided him in his work! What I should have noticed was how he was able to seamlessly integrate into the larger culture. Sure, you don't see many witches in public, but whatever being a witch meant to my coworker, it didn't affect his involvement in society. He could work, buy, eat, sleep, love, and have fun just like anyone else. In that sense, his persona was something added on to a standard life in a modern world.

If I had been paying attention, I would have realized that what the male witch was doing was the same as the rest of us in the electronics department. The only difference was that his cultivated image was a bit more exotic.

We all sought some kind of validation or fullness by playing, cultivating, and expressing an identity. The older salesmen never left the big-screen TV aisles. They prided themselves on their decades of service at Sears, their expertise in televisions, and their ability to close sales. They were family men who believed the good life did not require you to climb up the corporate ladder. It was enough to work hard in your position and support your family. The younger salespeople lacked this view.

Another salesman was working part time while attending a conservative Baptist Bible college in the area. For him, the good life involved personal piety, marriage, a family, and preaching the gospel. He had only recently "turned his life over to the Lord" after a youth of drinking and partying and sex. But now, he told me, he had given up such vices. His conception of the good life had changed so dramatically that he no longer even enjoyed going to the beach. He told me that all the women in swimsuits were a constant distraction for him, so he avoided the place entirely. I could empathize with the Baptist much better than with the male witch, but there was still a chasm between us. The Bible college student checked his progress toward a full life by constantly comparing himself to the sinful people around him. Even though he knew I was a Christian, I got the impression that he didn't think much of my faith. Where he saw himself as a solitary light in a wicked world, fighting off temptation and calling the world to repentance, I saw him as an insecure and anxious man. On slow nights we would hang out by the TVs talking, and I could watch while, in the middle of a sentence, his eyes would drift away from me to stare at women on the screens. My point here is not that the Baptist student was a hypocrite or prideful, but that we each had a conception of ourselves that formed our perception and experience of the world, so that even though we shared the same faith, we could hardly understand what drove the other person and where they were headed.

The other group in the electronics department were the apathetic young men. That's where I fit. None of us felt inspired by our work. Most of us were not very good at selling televisions. Whenever we could, we preferred to hang out—away from the career salespeople and the Bible student. For each of us, the good life meant something other than working at Sears. One guy wanted to be a firefighter or a scientist. Another wanted a comfortable job and to enjoy himself at parties, to be desired by women and envied by men. I didn't know exactly what I wanted to do, but I knew I wanted to do something *significant, impressive.* I wanted to accomplish something so great that I could feel my failure to sell TVs was because I was too smart and important to work sales at Sears. Even though I also struggled intensely with lust, I felt superior to the Bible student because at least I didn't blame women for wearing swimsuits at the beach. I felt superior to the career salespeople because, while I couldn't sell a TV to save my job, I never encouraged consumerism. If someone didn't need a bigger TV, I never tried to up-sell them. And most of all, I felt superior to the witch because I wasn't play-acting, unlike him—except that, in a sense, I was. Just like the male witch, I was obsessed with expressing my identity and finding some kind of existential justification through that expression.

What I couldn't see until much later was that we were all seeking our own sense of fullness in life. We each mapped our narrative of pursuing that fullness onto the world, a world that we all primarily or exclusively experienced as a closed, natural world. Our individual maps told us where we started, where we were, and where we were going. The legend pointed out the values and ideas that allowed us to make sense of our surroundings. But each map was different. And while I could speculate (and have) about how each of these salespeople conceived of the world, I could never really comprehend them, because the sources for our maps were ultimately *internal*. The maps came from deep within us, inspired by the external world, but always finally *chosen by us individually*. It's not that we were monads, unable to communicate what we believed to one another. Whatever ability we had to share glimpses of our personal worldview came from our constant signaling to each other about who we were. We were all interested in subtly letting each other know who we were and how to interpret us. And that's what the witch's cane was about. It was a physical symbol of his commitment to a way of seeing the world as magical and himself as a mage. The Bible student signaled with the small Bible he carried everywhere. The career salespeople signaled by ignoring the younger salespeople and talking about old times. The younger salespeople signaled with their disinterest in earning commissions and attending meetings. We expressed our identities to make our identities real.

While you may not have worked with a witch, what I've just described should be familiar to you. You should be able to identify examples of individually rooted quests for fullness in your own life and community. It may feel so ubiquitous that you can't even imagine another option: "Of course we all pursue our own vision of the good life, which we derive from sources within ourselves, the sources we believe are the most authentic. What's the alternative?"

There *is* an alternative way of conceiving of fullness and the good life: a shared cultural belief with transcendent origins. In this model, we don't measure our self-worth by an internal standard, we don't seek to identify our authentic individualism in order to fulfill it in practice, and we can't even conceive of a telos, or ultimate purpose, mapped from an internal source, because the nature of telos is that it exists outside of us and draws us to it. There isn't a simple answer for when and how this latter model of seeking purpose and fulfillment ceased to be the norm for Western culture. Certainly during the Middle Ages it was assumed, but building up to and during the twentieth century, Western civilization slowly shifted the locus of our hope from a transcendent source in God, who forms us, to finding it deep within ourselves. In no small part, explaining this shift is the goal of Charles Taylor's *A Secular Age*.

A SECULAR AGE

If the forces of technology and media alone affected our habits of thinking and believing, perhaps there would not be a serious need for us to alter the way we bear witness to our neighbors. But the barriers to belief created by technological and societal trends toward distraction have been dramatically strengthened by an increasing secularism in the West. Our secular age has produced an explosion of possible belief systems, all of which are endlessly contested and all of which make the idea of transcendent God less conceivable. As a result, our beliefs are more fragile and more individual, and less open to outside influence. We are buffered selves, protected behind a barrier of individual choice, rationalism, and a disenchanted world.

By *secularism* I don't mean "atheism," although atheism plays a role here. Instead, I'm using the term as defined by the Canadian Catholic philosopher Charles Taylor, who has argued that we live in a "secular age," which differs from the past not in that most people do not believe in God but that not believing in God is a live option: "The shift to secularity in this sense consists, among other things, of a move from a society where belief in God is unchallenged and indeed, unproblematic, to one in which it is understood to be one option among others, and frequently not the easiest to embrace."[1] In the secular age, all sorts of beliefs are live options. The one truth we accept about belief in our secular age is that there is an endless number of options, and all of them are contested. In addition, our understanding of these beliefs tends to be more "fragile" than beliefs held in the past.[2] Whereas people traditionally kept the beliefs of their parents and community, today it is normal and even expected for each contemporary individual in the West to choose their own, personal beliefs. And it is common for people to change beliefs multiple times over their lives.[3] Because all beliefs are contested and we are hyperaware of other options, our commitment to any one belief tends to be much looser. We have witnessed a corresponding decline in all of the structural forces that helped define and enforce belief in the past. Institutions are weaker. We are less reliant on founding documents or philosophies. There are fewer authorities governing right belief. Belief itself is flattened and shifted to the inner judgment of the individual.

Part of the reason we can hold our beliefs so lightly is that what is truly important to us is not only or primarily our beliefs but how they affect our identity. Identity formation becomes the central concern, and our beliefs are just another way we articulate that identity. Since we hold these beliefs loosely, we have less cognitive dissonance when picking and choosing beliefs that contradict one another. A lack of reflection makes it easier for us to hold contradictory beliefs, but now we see that our secular age contributes to this condition by leveling beliefs.

At the heart of the secular age is the individual in their effort to create and project their identity in a chaotic and hostile world.[4] For Christians this means that open dialogue about the merits and truth of the Christian faith can all too easily be interpreted by our hearers as reasons why they should choose to add Christianity to their identity. And then reasoning about the faith becomes futile, because their objections to Christianity are not so much logical as existential: the faith (if properly described) simply does not *fit* with their conception of themselves. And so they may reply, "Christianity just isn't my thing."

The issue is not that modern people do not think rationally about faith. Reason is one of the defining features of modernity, and more than ever people trust that through reason, logic, and science we can perfect our knowledge and progress as humans. But we assume that the proper object of reason is the practical, physical world. This is why atheists' arguments about the net harm of religion or studies reporting that children who are raised in a religious home are less kind are so persuasive to modern ears. The proper realm of reason, the assumption goes, is the sensible world, and the goal of reason is to live a more comfortable, safe, and happy life. Thus, arguments that show how ineffective or harmful religion is carry a lot of weight.

Such arguments imply that the real criteria for the validity of a belief system is how quantifiably beneficial it is to us, personally. (This understanding of reason stands in stark contrast to older conceptions of it, like we find in Dante's *Divine Comedy*, where reason is the first necessary guide toward Christ.) And because reason can be so thoroughly separated from faith, when we have frank and rational discussions of Christianity, it may be that we are not arguing about a religion with a transcendent referent but a potentially effective belief for *this* world. In that sense, the historical case for the resurrection is less important to a hearer than "Would adopting Christianity fit with and improve my authentic identity?" or "Would this faith improve my quality of life?"

I am speaking in generalities here about large cultural trends. There are exceptions. Perhaps you have even thought of a few rational conversations you have had with non-Christians about the faith that you believe were effective in bearing witness. It's not that providing reasons and evidence is foolish; they have a place and a purpose in the way we share our faith. Rather, our culture's default way of interpreting religious claims is via the assumption that any religion is just one option among many. We imagine that they all have *some* truth to them, so that what matters most is how a religion fits with who we envision ourselves to be. Thus the criteria for belief shifts from external ideals to internal ones, and that, in part, is what it means to be a buffered self.

EVERYTHING IS CONTESTED

How belief in a God-created cosmos ceased to be a basic, accepted background truth for people in the West is long, complicated, and debated. In fact, Charles Taylor's *A Secular Age*, all eight hundred–plus pages, is devoted to answering the question, "Why was it virtually impossible not to believe in God in, say, 1500 in our Western society, while in 2000 many of us find this not only easy, but even inescapable?"[5] Traditionally, Taylor tell us, the story of the secularization of the West has been told as a "subtraction story." In the 1500s it was hard *not* to believe in God because we understood the world as a part of a cosmos created by God, society was ordered in reference to God, and the world was enchanted because a transcendent God created it. But then, slowly, we saw the physical world more as part of a universe that could be explained through science, without recourse to God. Society could be ordered through reason and an understanding of human rights. Belief in spirits and supernatural forces was viewed as childish superstition, and so the world became disenchanted.[6]

Once religion was "subtracted," we were left with just our own ability to interpret and order our world: exclusive humanism. Taylor rejects this subtraction, in part because it assumes that exclusive humanism is simply our natural worldview rather than something we had to learn.[7] But since we learned it, our society has seen an explosion in the number of plausible beliefs, and they are all contested.

Western culture experienced a profound shift inward during the Enlightenment and the Reformation, a shift that prioritized the individual as the basic arbiter of truth. A moral dimension is added to individualism. Rather than depending on tradition, the church, the king, or your community to order your life, now you are morally obligated to search out the truth and verify it for yourself. Along with this comes a skepticism and criticism of the foundational and formative institutions of society: the church, the state, and traditions. It is not that people abandon these authorities, but they no longer assume these forces are valid and correct. Instead, they are just more contested institutions. Whereas in 1350, if you lived in Europe you were almost certainly part of the Catholic Church, by 1550 you might be a member of any number of churches, each claiming supremacy. Later, deism expanded the belief horizons even further, a process that has continued to today. The result is that as strongly as you hold your beliefs, you are aware that they aren't *really* the only option. Maybe you leave the Catholic Church after reading about Martin Luther's criticisms, but you don't have to become Lutheran. You can join Calvin's Reformed Church, or the Anabaptists, or the English Puritans, and with each passing decade as the options multiply, people increasingly *feel* the pressure of living in a contested space. This is the experience of what Charles Taylor means by secularism: the constant background sense that there are any number of possible beliefs, and many of them involve no reference to a transcendent being.[8]

In some ways, Western society has turned this experience of tentative belief into a virtue, which is significant because with the collapse of a shared belief system we lost a shared stable of virtues to aspire to. Being open-minded, refusing to draw conclusions, the idea that diversity of belief is a good unto itself—these are all results of a fundamental shift in our basic beliefs about the world. Thus, we *aspire* to be noncommittal.

We see the modern virtue of uncertainty play out even in the way people come to faith. For example, when we hear that a Christian was raised in the faith, modern hearers are tempted to question their sincerity. Are they *really* Christian or did they just happen to be raised that way? Have they considered the alternatives? The church tries to alleviate the anxiety of being raised in the faith by relying on testimonies to suss out true believers. So it is common for evangelicals to have to present their testimony when applying to work in ministry or when joining a new church or Bible study. The cradle Christian feels pressure to discover a story of sin and redemption, usually somewhere in the distant past, as evidence of their authentic faith.

In other words, being raised from childhood into belief in Christ is suspicious, somehow less genuine, and certainly more susceptible to a falling away because the alternatives have not been considered. Rather than seeing faithfulness from birth to death as a blessing from God (which is certainly the model of the Old Testament), we harbor doubts about such believers' sincerity. On the other hand, the ideal model is someone who reaches adulthood, studies all the religions and worldviews they can, weighs the evidence, and decides that Christianity is the truth.

The description of modern belief I have just given might sound as if it results in philosophical relativism, the belief that everyone's reality is true insofar as it is true for them. But this would be a mistake. For one, people do not always go to the logical conclusions of their beliefs. So, even modern people who feel deeply that all beliefs are contested may never come to the conclusion that all beliefs are equally valid. This may never occur to them! Indeed, such relativism is hard to maintain; we are constantly reminded of positions and views that are not only contrary to our own but also deeply offensive and obviously harmful. We should expect modern people, including Christians, to hold strongly to their beliefs and even reject alternatives as falsehoods, but here is the crucial difference for the modern period: no matter how *confident* we modern people are in our worldview, we are always aware of the alternatives. As a result, we become increasingly concerned with signaling our beliefs. For example, no small part of what it means to be a Christian involves our internal and external identification with Christian culture so we know our place in relation to the rest of the world. Our focus shifts away from practicing our beliefs to signaling our beliefs to ourselves and others. In a world where all beliefs are possible, our attention turns to contending about beliefs, and the terms and conditions of those beliefs matter less, except as fodder. Is it any wonder that apologetics is so difficult?

You may be wondering at this point, how can Christians escape this modern, secular view of endless options for belief in our world? It may not be possible or even desirable to escape. In fact, the early church context was somewhat similar to our own (only with fewer options for belief). The fact that we are aware of many other ways of living and seeking fulfillment does not necessarily undermine our faith, but secularism subtly causes problems for the church and our witness. Rather than reverse secularism (which I don't think is possible until the Lord returns), our task is to identify the harmful outcomes of secularism and reject them.

One of those outcomes is the tendency to focus intensely on the contestedness of our belief, identifying with it rather than practicing the belief. Another disordered outcome is our unconscious privileging of adult converts over cradle Christians. Secularism is more a fact about our modern situation than an enemy to be overcome. But this fact has effects that must be tested against the truth of the Bible. This book is one such test.

The contestedness of belief points us inward, rather than outward, for the basis or ground of our being. If the external world appears to be an endless series of options, from deodorant brands to philosophies, our temptation is to withdraw to a safe, seemingly stable world—the inner world of our being. Our identity and our ability to choose its features becomes the basis for our being in the world, rather than some outside authority. So that even when we believe in God's existence and choose to follow him, we do so because of an inner decision (the buffered self!).

THIN BELIEF

While the secular age does not necessarily lead to philosophical relativism, it does lead to thin belief. By "thin belief" I mean a set of foundational ideas about the world that lack robust explan-atory power. Their sources may be obscured from us, consciously or not. They may come in direct conflict with other beliefs we hold (more on that later). In a sense, all of our beliefs are part of a continuum from thick beliefs (which involve a deep under-standing of the internal logic, origins, and context; embodied practice; and robust application of the belief) to thin beliefs (which can be as superficial as signaling your support for a po-litical cause simply because you like its hashtag). We hold a thin belief when we fail to grasp its assorted justifications and rea-sonings, and therefore are unable to articulate it fully. We then struggle to consistently live according to it. Thin beliefs are easy to adopt and then toss away, so they are useful for crafting our self-image. Not that the beliefs themselves necessarily lack depth, tradition, passion, or truth. In fact, this is part of the great shame of thin belief: it may affect otherwise good beliefs, mistreating and misrepresenting them.

We can adopt thin beliefs about almost anything. Perhaps you become deeply convicted about the plight of Syrian refugees after the US president callously calls for them to be banned. His words strike you as offensive, inhumane, and cruel. And while you may still harbor some unspoken suspicions about Middle Easterners after 9/11, this issue feels like the perfect opportunity to show your goodwill. The next time you see a meme showing refugee children with a superimposed verse about caring for the "least of these," you decide not only to like it but to *share* it with your friends. This signals what your stance is on the issue and maybe something about your personal character, your open-mindedness and concern for foreigners. An argument breaks out on your post, with some of your distant relatives and old high school friends arguing over whether Islam is a religion of peace and whether "moderate Muslims" exist. You jump in to defend your position, citing lines of argument that you've picked up from other viral images or a John Oliver clip you watched on YouTube. You care about this issue passionately. There is a tremendous moral urgency to your writing, and you are even willing to anger and lose friends over your stance—a stance you adopted fifteen minutes prior, after seeing a compelling viral image on Facebook. Meanwhile, the foundation of your belief goes unquestioned.

You could consider the procedural issue of risk analysis (how likely is it that one of these refugees turns out to be an ISIS member who commits a deadly terrorist attack?), but the moral source of your belief remains unspoken and unidentified. What ethical obligation do we have to our international neighbors? What does this mean for other global conflicts? What does this ethic mean for military interventions and global trade and climate agreements? What shape should a local community take, and how can and should it adapt to foreign newcomers? The web of complex ethical questions that shapes the debate over Syrian refugees matters a great deal, but it's unlikely that you will explore these questions. Why? Aside from the technological pressure to move on to the "next thing," which we discussed in chapter one, there is also the feeling that there are just too many important issues for us to care about. The best we can do is stand for *something*. And once we commit to a cause, its momentum sweeps us along.

We've all felt this when arguing some controversial issue online. There is a moral urgency to defend our cause. And if we are honest, no small part of that urgency involves unarticulated fears about how losing this argument might reflect on *our image*. We need to defend refugees not only because they need defending but because we want to be the kind of people who are *known* for defending refugees. This becomes evident when we step back and realize that our online defense of refugees is highly unlikely to *actually* defend them in practice. But because this is a thin belief, this won't bother us much. We're already on to the next cause.

So, a political and moral cause is adopted uncritically. The adoption of the belief primarily takes the form of public expression (your concern for refugees is not likely to stay in the realm of quiet prayers). You are aware that this expression signals things about yourself to others. You defend this belief passionately, despite having little understanding of the deeper ethical motivations. And you know that ultimately your defense is for the benefit of you and your friends, a kind of image-crafting game we play. Meanwhile, refugees are still in crisis.[9]

We aren't all just heartless egotists who use the sufferings of others as props for our expressive individualism. I'm sure that's true for some people, but it is hardly the norm. Instead, we see the formation of an identity as part of our moral duty, and formation takes place, as Charles Taylor argues in his book *The Ethics of Authenticity*, in dialogue with others.[10] This is how we sharpen and declare our beliefs. But when we sincerely and passionately hold thin beliefs, we often do so in conflict with other thin beliefs, and we are liable to drop them when the next issue comes along. Our modern world invites us to adopt thin beliefs whose moral foundations are poorly understood and which serve in no small way to tell others about who we are, rather than, necessarily, to affect some actual change in some human condition.

Thin belief does not mean that we no longer hold any strong, deep beliefs. On the contrary, most of us have a few beliefs we identify with strongly and that have deep roots, but because we are hyperaware of the contestedness of the world, we are more inclined to hold a strange mixture of thin and thick beliefs, even within the same larger belief system. And the way we express our beliefs to others may make no noticeable distinction between thick and thin beliefs. (Our favorite sports team is listed right along with our marital and parental status and occupation in our Twitter bio.) For example, let's say that Reformed Christianity is one of the thick, strong beliefs that defines me, but sometimes I find partaking in the weekly Lord's Supper at my Presbyterian church to be tedious. Since I am aware of the diversity of beliefs within Christianity, even within Reformed tradition, I might wonder about how often we should celebrate the Lord's Supper, and since I'm also aware that most of my neighbors would say that the entire debate is unimportant, I might not feel all that motivated to come to a conclusion. The diversity of views on the Lord's Supper invites me to throw my hands up in resignation and follow my personal preferences. If I do decide to come to a conclusion, the pressure of all the alternative views will drive me to devote myself to intense study and defense of a particular view, as if my faith depended on certainty on this issue. Certain beliefs like this within larger belief systems may be thinly understood and loosely held, even while the broader belief system itself is thick and strong.

The image of belief that I would like you to envision is one in which spots of thick belief are surrounded by thin beliefs and everything in between, in an uneven, unordered design. The good news is that our hope in Christ is not based on having a perfectly coherent and thoroughly understood belief in Christ and the world he created. God's grace covers our sins, our doubts, and our ignorance. It is based on Christ's righteousness, not our comprehensively understood doctrine. But we ought to work toward an awareness of what we believe and why we believe it. Which brings us to another major feature of secularism: the un-critical embrace of contrary beliefs about the world.

CONTRARY BELIEFS

No one lives out their beliefs consistently. We all have little pockets of preferences or desires or practices that rub up against what we would claim to be our basic morals and beliefs. Memory, knowledge, will, and sin prevent us from properly living out our worldview. And this has always been true. But the kind of inner conflict between different beliefs that I am describing is much more intense than standard human hy-pocrisy. Because we are hyperaware of the endless choices in beliefs, and because we are inclined to hold thin beliefs loosely, our tendency is to form a collection of hodgepodge beliefs about the world—beliefs that would be seen as incoherent if we were to look closely at them and their implications, but we don't. Or at least we try not to. And so our perception of the world shifts easily as we gain new information, new desires, and new influences. We are unmoored.

A strange consequence of this flattening of values is that the distance grows shorter between a belief about our origins, for example, and a belief about who is the greatest basketball player of all time. We understand that both beliefs are tenuous and contentious and identity defining, and so in some respects we may hold each of them just as fervently. We may become apologists for both beliefs. We may purchase clothes to identify with both. We allocate time and money to both.

To illustrate what having a collection of conflicting beliefs might look like, let's start with the way evangelicals often talk about beliefs in terms of discrete "worldviews." A worldview is commonly understood as a holistic way of interpreting the world and our position in it. Worldviews are regularly divided into a number of major headings, such as humanism, Marxism, Islam, biblical Christianity, postmodernism, pragmatism, Darwinism, and so on. This way of understanding belief assumes that we primarily come to belief through conscious, cognitive choice.[11] We reason about the world and our experience and draw conclusions that lead us to one of the major worldviews. When this assumption is paired with the claim that "ideas have consequences," the result is that we may assume a great deal about what people believe in the particulars and how they will act if we can "read" their worldview.

Worldviews can be used in different ways. For instance, there is a predictive function of worldview. I was taught that if I met a self-identifying postmodernist, I could expect them to deny reality because, after all, postmodernism teaches that the binary distinctions between truth and falsehood collapse under inspection. (This is a reductive account of a notoriously hard-to-define philosophy—but it is also the kind of reductive understanding of ideologies I've seen taught under the banner of "worldview" studies.) Worldview studies also have an inductive function—if we can observe enough about a person or a cultural work, we can determine which worldview box they fit into. From here, we may compare the secular worldview with the Christian one and see how the former fails. Finally, there's an explanatory function of worldview. For example, I have seen the following argument made by fellow evangelicals countless times: If we know someone to be a liberal politician and we catch them in a lie, we can *explain* their lie as a natural and logical outgrowth of their belief that truth is a function of power. Whereas when a conservative Christian politician lies, we conclude that the lie was not actually a consequence of their belief but in spite of it. It seems that ideas have consequences, except when they have the wrong ones.

Whatever the merits and demerits of worldview studies, the popular understanding of worldview analysis easily leads to lazy and misguided thinking about how people actually experience and interpret the world.[12] This not a necessary slide, but it is a common one. The very structure of worldview studies pushes us to draw hasty conclusions about actual people. An experiential understanding of worldview would be much more accurate, in which we would need to include everything a person experiences, because a true "world view" is utterly comprehensive and infinitely detailed and ultimately untraceable. A bad breakup in sixth grade, the death of your father, your favorite band, and your experience as a prematurely bald man will have deep effects on you, just as will your parents' conservative politics and your school's teaching on origins, maybe even more so. Witnessing a relative abuse the welfare system to fund a methamphetamine addiction or having to rely on food stamps to feed your own family for a while can both deeply alter your beliefs about the state's role in providing aid. The way humans view the world is always necessarily embodied, and it includes a perception of reality strongly formed by our past experiences.

Worldviews are composed of all the data we receive in life, and no less. James K. A. Smith has demonstrated that traditional worldview studies overemphasize rational, intentional, and cognitive beliefs over the way habits shape our desires. I'd add that our experience of being is just as formative as how we perceive reality; and liturgy, experience, memories, and even personality are largely ignored by worldview studies. Which means that a true worldview is irreducible to categories. In this sense, Marxism was *only* a worldview for Marx. What we call Marxism is not really a worldview at all but a broad ideology or belief about people, history, and governments. It may or may not have widespread implications for most areas of life, but those implications often will not materialize. Because, while ideas have consequences, they do not *necessarily* have consequences. And they never have the kind of *totalizing* consequences implied by the term *worldview*.

To be fair, some of the best worldview thinkers are aware of these dangers. Where I disagree with them most is on the practical question of the effectiveness of this method. Whereas worldview thinkers will argue that speaking in terms of the humanist or environmentalist worldview gives us new insight into people and their beliefs, I contend that in practice worldview studies lack explanatory power and often misinterpret people. This is increasingly true today when the fundamental contestedness of all belief and the tendency toward thin belief have conspired to incline us to form eclectic mixes of belief, something we are often quite proud of because it separates us as individuals: I may take a bit of Marxist economics, a conservative view on family and sex and virtues, a modern empirical view of the natural world, a view of nature as raw material for human use, libertarian politics (except on economics), and then undergird it all with a Reformed faith. Would such a worldview be coherent? Probably not, but maybe it makes its own kind of sense to me and how I perceive myself. This means that the language of worldview has increasingly less value. Instead, we ought to speak about general ideologies that individuals hold to varying extents at different times.

How can we hold such a motley collection of perceptions and ideas together without great cognitive dissonance? To some extent, we can't. And we don't. Instead we continually jettison some ideas and adopt others, so there is rarely time for sustained, thorough reflection about what we believe to be true about the world. A shifting sand can never be measured for angle. To whatever extent that we hold these contrary beliefs without troubling dissonance, it is because we feel that there will always be dissonance. That ache in our stomach that we are wrong about something doesn't really disappear, no matter what. Because even if we somehow found better, more consistent beliefs, we would always feel that external pressure to consider some *other* idea.

When the natural state of mind is the pressing awareness that there's always one more viewpoint to consider, that we *might* be wrong, we grow used to dissonance. No matter what we believe, we will be ignoring some contrary evidence. In the secular age, cognitive dissonance is the normal state of things.

INNER DEPTHS

What then holds us together? What could possibly overcome a perpetual sense that our perception of the world is potentially wrong and needs correction? What would allow us to accept the contestedness of existence? In a response that in some ways echoes René Descartes's beginning quest for certainty, our answer is often a move toward what Charles Taylor calls "inner depths." By this he means the vast, mysterious complexity of our personal psyche: "We might even say that the depths which were previously located in the cosmos, the enchanted world, are now more readily placed within."[13] When overwhelmed by the infinite iterations of belief that call into question our knowledge and belief, we find the ground to being in our choices. We may not know what is *true*, but we know with certainty that it is our task to *choose* what we believe to be true and that choice will define us publicly. Choice then becomes foregrounded, the choice of the individual.

We may be tempted to conclude that this is the sin of narcissism, and therefore if we can convict people of their selfishness, all these corresponding problems will go away. But Charles Taylor thinks something more than crass egotism is at work.[14] It may *lead* to narcissism in many cases, but the condition I've just described involves something more fundamental. It is a reflexive way of understanding being in the world.

The secular age turns everything back to the self. During the Middle Ages in the West, you were born in a specific social, economic, religious, gender, political, and commercial position. You had a place within the Great Chain of Being, which led from God all the way down to rocks and dirt. When you came of age, you were not expected to search out your identity, decide which political party to join, or whether to believe in God or which God. Almost without exception, these things were chosen for you.

The modern era stands in stark contrast to this, and the secular age is the culmination of modernity. Together, secularism and the technology of distraction work to place the telos of belief in the individual person. That is, the end purpose of beliefs, the future goal we devote ourselves to achieving, is the fulfillment of the self. We choose the beliefs that comprise our particular worldview (here the word is applicable) based principally on what will grant us a sense of personal fulfillment or self-actualization. Thus, to make decisions on what we will think about the world, we need to look inward. What will help me make sense of the world? What will give me purpose? What will make me happy?

STUCK IN AN IMMANENT FRAME

Framing all these new conceptions of belief is the background sense that we live in an entirely natural, material, explicable, measurable, and comprehensible world. Taylor calls this the immanent frame: "The buffered identity of the disciplined individual moves in a constructed social space, where instrumental rationality is a key value, and time is pervasively secular. All of this makes up what I want to call the 'immanent frame.'"[15] The immanent frame comes in different forms. It is possible to feel that we live in a closed immanent frame, which means that there is no higher, transcendent reality. The material universe we live in is all there is and ever will be. But it is also possible to experience life within an *open* immanent frame.[16] By this Taylor means that although our daily experience isn't imbued with the supernatural, we believe that some transcendent being exists and that he can break into our world at certain times and places. What is notable here is that even when the immanent frame is open, it is still the immanent frame.

To get a sense of what this look likes, consider for a minute what it is like to attend church on Sunday. You are awakened by an alarm on your cell phone, an amazing piece of technology and testament to the power of human mastery over the natural world. You eat eggs for breakfast. They come, almost miraculously, clean, large, and white in a carton that has been inspected by some government agency to ensure it is safe. The carton lists the nutritional composition of the eggs along with a few words about their health benefits. Everything has been considered. You get dressed in clothes that you bought ready-made. You drive to church in a glistening, energy-efficient sedan with advanced safety features, and glance occasionally at the cars next to you, in which people are completely preoccupied and content with the technology around them. As you drive through the city, everything you see appears as a work of human achievement: stoplights, fire trucks, businesses, freeway overpasses, and skyscrapers. By chance you see a bluebird, and you immediately reflect back on a recent episode of an animal show you watched that featured the bluebird. "Bluebirds are part of the thrush family," you say to no one in particular. At church, you sing songs praising God's provision, his mercies, his creation, and his grace. But everything you experienced on the way to church, from the food you ate to the beauty you witnessed, testified to humanity's ingenuity and mastery of the world. Your *experience* of the world was a testament to humanity, not God, because everything in your experience conditioned you to look to this world and its physical laws. It all makes sense as a self-sufficient immanent world, even though you know that Jesus is our Creator and Sustainer. And so, we experience life in the immanent frame even as we confess that it is open to an outside, transcendent force.

While it's possible for us to believe in a transcendent God and still live within the immanent frame, it isn't easy. In fact, it's becoming increasingly difficult. As the previous example illustrated, providence, mystery, contingency, uncertainty, wonder, and randomness have been systematically, bureaucratically, technologically, and economically drained from our world. Living in such a world makes it difficult to conceive of being outside the immanent frame. Most of us do not rely on good weather for our livelihood or sustenance. We struggle to recognize beauty in the natural world because it has been so thoroughly conquered, and wonder is quashed through scientific language and nature-channel explainers. We are masters of our health, our safety, our morality, our time, and our success. Living in this kind of society, it is hard to *sense* the transcendent. It seems superfluous. This situation is so pervasive that when we bear witness to our faith to a non-Christian, they may imagine the faith as just another belief system within a closed immanent frame.

And herein lies another barrier to belief. The Christian faith requires a belief in a risen and living Savior, one who lived in this immanent world and transcended it both on the cross and in his ascension. But for our neighbors, the experience of modern life is something like what Peter described in 2 Peter 3:4: "They will say, 'Where is the promise of his coming? For ever since the fathers fell asleep, all things are continuing as they were from the beginning of creation.'" The world simply does not feel like a place where the supernatural intervenes. The cognitive barrier facing us is, How do we speak to people who feel that things are continuing as they have from the beginning? Who believe that the divine doesn't interrupt our lives and there will be no second coming to interrupt this march of mechanical time. Our witness must work to disrupt the normative experience of life in a closed immanent frame.

CONCLUSION

Combining Taylor's understanding of secularism with the technological culture described in chapter one, we may draw some startling conclusions. First, *how* we believe is determined by how we articulate our personal identification with a belief. There is less and less separation between believing something and publicly identifying with that belief. Second, *why* we believe is determined by the ability of a set of beliefs to give us a sense of fullness or the *promise* of fullness. Third, *what* we believe is determined not by coherence or correspondence to truth but by expediency.

Fourth, *when* we discuss our beliefs, in a sense we are able to gamble both more and less than people in similar positions in premodern worlds. We gamble more in the sense that we are aware that everything is contested and so we *expect* our beliefs to be publicly challenged, and we freely offer them up for debate. But we gamble less in the sense that these beliefs are thin and lightly held. Regardless of the course of the debate, our lives will not *fundamentally* change.

Our path to fullness is determined internally. If we happen to adopt a path taught by a religion, it is only because we have chosen to, not because we are compelled to by an external authority. As Taylor notes, "For many people today, to set aside their own path in order to conform to some external authority just doesn't seem comprehensible as a form of spiritual life."[17] Our journey may involve us wearing various "hats of belief," but the journey itself lasts as long as we do, and so our choices constitute the form our journey takes, but perhaps little else.

The implications of all this for evangelism and witness bearing are vast. What we intend to be a persuasive proclamation of the gospel may instead be interpreted by our neighbor as an expression of our identity through argument, just like any other dialogue in modern culture. Our conversation isn't *really* about someone named Jesus Christ who was the Son of God and who died for our sins; it is about you publicly defining yourself as a Christian through debate because it gives you a certain sense of personal fulfillment and because of your need to promote that definition. I may try on Christianity like I try on styles of clothes or beliefs, but the ultimate focus of this conversation is not an external being who loves me but my own search for fullness. The challenge, in other words, is that rational arguments for the existence of God, scholarly defenses of the reliability of Scripture, or even personal testimonies of the effectiveness of Christianity in transforming our lives all seamlessly fit into the fluid market of ideas within secularism. Secularism can shape-shift, absorbing counternarratives with ease, since it assumes that every belief is endlessly contested.

This calls for a different way of bearing witness to the gospel of Christ. We need a method of living in light of the gospel that unsettles people from their stupor. The way we communicate our faith must puncture the buzz of modern life, the thinness of belief, the closed immanent frame, and our attempts at crafting identities and narratives of our own.

Talking about Christ's death and resurrection for our sins is categorically different than talking about the importance of conservative politics or the pleasure of some musical album. But if we are born into a culture that sees belief as first a performance of identity and thus something we can easily slip on or off, then it's only natural that when we share the gospel we will be inclined to treat it as a performance of our identity.

3

SEARCHING FOR VISIONS OF FULLNESS

B oth secularism and distraction have the effect of scrambling us, inclining us toward frail, fragmented, and incoherent beliefs, and making it difficult for us to communicate the full weight and exclusiveness of the gospel. This insight should raise questions for us about how modern people cope. Given the distracted and secular age we inhabit, how do most Americans, including Christians, find meaning and justification in life? How can we build a vision of fullness in a world of frail, fragmented, and incoherent beliefs? If we cannot answer this question, we will not truly understand the modern condition and how the gospel of Jesus Christ is a profound challenge to it.

Perhaps even more concerning, if we are not aware of how a distracted and secular age shapes us and inclines us to look for meaning in life, then we will not be able to see the ways Christians have wrongly adopted unbiblical and impoverished ideals. Our faith has the resources to overcome the challenges of our times, but the church has often left those resources untapped.

Distraction and secularism have shaped the way modern people tend to find or create meaning in their lives. First, a culture of technological distraction inclines us to look for meaning in preoccupation, novelty, consumer choices, and stimulation. So long as we are moving on to the next thing, we feel that our life has some direction and therefore meaning. There is a nearly limitless number of images of fullness to choose from, and a person can be expected to change their ideal of fullness several times over the course of their life. So, it may be more accurate to talk about someone's meanings of life. Second, the immanent frame inclines modern people to try to find sources of fulfillment without recourse to any transcendent source. Put differently, we can find meaning and a kind of justification without needing a god, an ideal, a being, or a universal principle to define and verify our lives. Third, broadly speaking, our society embraces *expressive individualism*, a term that describes the modern idea that we gain meaning and justification in life through our individual identity, and we establish our identity through self-expression. Charles Taylor writes that "there arises in Western societies a generalized culture of 'authenticity,' or expressive individualism, in which people are encouraged to find their own way, discover their own fulfillment, 'do their own thing.'"[1] To go beyond these ideas and flesh out how meaning and justification are commonly gained in the modern world, we should begin with the set of tensions that create the desire for fullness. This is not meant to be an exhaustive or uncontroversial exploration of this desire, but it will help shape our understanding of meaning and justification—two terms that will become clearer as we look at these motivating tensions.

WHAT WE DESIRE FROM FULLNESS

Life is miraculous. As adults, that miraculousness weighs on us. But children naturally perceive and delight in the irreducible wonder of life. Observe a toddler's joy in simply walking or jumping. My nearly two-year-old daughter can hardly get both of her feet off the ground when she jumps. It looks more like skipping in place, and half the time she lands on her bottom. But when she is "jumping," she can hardly contain her pleasure, because her body is amazing. Her pure excitement overwhelms my wife and me—we can't help but cheer her on, even though her jumping is, technically speaking, pretty sad. In these moments the praise we give is not feigned praise for her jumping; we praise her for taking delight in the goodness of being. This is the same praise we give her when she hands us a dandelion as if it were the most precious flower in the universe. That's the only kind of flower a little girl ever gives to her parents. Our gratitude is not condescending, but a brief acknowledgment that at some level she is able to see the wonder in the world that we have become numb to. On some level she is right; it is the most precious flower in the universe.

Ernest Becker wrote of this dynamic in his book *The Denial of Death*.

> The world as it *is*, creation out of the void, things as they are, things as they are not, are too much for us to be able to stand. Or, better: they *would be* too much for us to bear without crumbling in a faint, trembling like a leaf, standing in a trance *in response* to the movement, colors, and orders of the world. I say "would be" because most of us—by the

time we leave childhood—have repressed our vision of the primary miraculousness of creation. We have closed it off, changed it, and no longer perceive the world as it is to raw experience. Sometimes we may recapture this world by remembering some striking childhood perceptions, how suffused they were in emotion and wonder—how a favorite grandfather looked, or one's first love in his early teens. We change these heavily emotional perceptions precisely because we need to move about in the world with some kind of equanimity, some kind of strength and directness; we can't keep gaping with our heart in our mouth, greedily sucking up with our eyes everything great and powerful that strikes us. The great boon of repression is that it makes it possible to live decisively in an overwhelmingly miraculous and incomprehensible world, a world so full of beauty, majesty, and terror that if animals perceived it all they would be paralyzed to act.[2]

The burden of existence calls for a commensurate justification of our being. The fact that we are alive, that we have agency, that we are capable of such tremendous heights and depths emotionally, that our minds have such a capacity for love and creation and reason, that our subjective experiences appear to have irreducible meaning and value despite the fact that they are subjective—all of these things burden us. The beauty and goodness of our particular being demands some justification: What right do I have to such a life? Without a justification, we feel like phonies, frauds, failures, or, at best, lost.

Here's how we might experience the burden of existence. Imagine you and your lover take a walk one evening after dinner. Nothing particularly intimate is said. It's mostly small talk broken by periods of silence pregnant with mutual longing and satisfaction in each other. The air is unusually still and cool, and the streets are quiet. And then you go home.

When you look back on that night, days or weeks or years later, you won't be able to articulate why it meant so much to you. But there is a feeling that during that walk you experienced something beautiful and good, something that only you in that specific moment with that specific person in that specific place could experience. And it wasn't merely the uniqueness of the experience that gave it weight. The purely empirical, statistical fact that your experience was one-of-a-kind has no bearing here. You experienced a moment that revealed the goodness of being alive, of feeling and loving and sensing. It was the experience of semiconsciously making a million connections between memories and daydreams and smells and hopes and words, spoken and unspoken. Every tiny, uncountable sensation on that walk felt, in some cosmic sense, right. The position of every bird. Every sound. The warmth of your lover's hands in yours. The green of the leaves. The sound of grass and dirt and gravel beneath your feet. The particularity of being alive right then.

This is the burden of being. And it's only a burden because it is irreducibly beautiful and good. It forces the question: Why me? What can possibly explain the incredible splendor of my existence? How can we understand this goodness in light of the horrors and sufferings in this world?

I chose an image of romantic love because it is one of the most universal reference points for modern people, but we can experience the same burden of existence by ourselves, watching a cat sleep peacefully in the sunlight, or listening to a beautiful song, or choosing to show mercy to someone. There is no end to the possibilities.

This tension doesn't arise only for those who have experienced romantic love or live pleasant lives or can afford nice things. In some ways, the tension is all the greater for those who are suffering abuse, oppression, and unusual pain in life. They too recognize the immensity of their consciousness, the power of their agency in the world, their immeasurable capacity for wonder and gratitude, but they have been deprived of the opportunities to flourish. And that injustice creates an ache or an anger: Why me? How can I be capable of such ineffable things and yet be so cruelly deprived of them?

Even in those moments when we loathe ourselves, when we despair of our very lives, we recognize that our life has significance that is utterly irreducible to our achievements, personality, success, education, characteristics, and righteousness.

As Ernest Becker notes, we stifle the miraculousness of the world in order to move freely within it. This is part of what it means to be a buffered self. We protect ourselves from the external power of the givenness of existence. Instead, the power is felt to reside entirely in our heads and can therefore be chosen or dismissed. When we experience a beautiful sunset, the sunset is only the occasion for us to create a judgment of beauty in our heads. But if there is a goodness and meaning to creation that is truly external, then that meaning exists independent to us. Although Becker argues that we repress the world of "beauty, majesty, and terror," I suspect he would agree that, as with most repression, it is never completely successful. We still have moments when the wonder of the world disrupts our buffered self. And when repression is successful, it requires a narrative, some story to explain away the miraculous. In one way or another, we all must find a way to justify our existence in the world, to offer some validation, some evidence that explains why we are. It is, in some ways, a terrifying burden. Felt against the background of a cold, indifferent, impersonal universe, our being can only be explained as an illusion of evolution—an accident of the development of consciousness. But for most of us, that is not a satisfying answer, so we will look elsewhere.

The desire for existential justification is related to the desire for meaning in our lives. We want to know that the significance of our personal existence is justified, but we also want to know that it has meaning that extends over time and place and circumstances. To live a life of meaning is to have an interpretive framework for explaining how our significance relates to the rest of existence. Specifically, we desire to be oriented toward some telos, some ultimate purpose that provides coherence, moral guidance, trajectory, explanation, and vitality to our lives. Another way to understand our telos is as an ultimate good to which we are oriented, like truth, justice, or love. For Charles Taylor, orientation toward some good gives our life meaning: "We come here to one of the most basic aspirations of human beings, the need to be connected to, or in contact with, what they see as good, or of crucial importance, or of fundamental value."[3] This telos will also typically act as the source for our personal justification, so that we move toward some vision of goodness while feeling our experience of goodness justified. We say our life has meaning when we have a strong sense of what our life is building toward and when that sense provides adequate moral, aesthetic, and existential significance to our actions. A vision of fullness is a way of imagining how to give our lives meaning and justification.

The dominant way the desire for existential justification and meaning has tended to take shape in late twentieth and early twenty-first centuries is as a generic existentialist philosophy. (Existentialism is a complex and diverse movement, but it generally involves the belief that "existence precedes essence" and that meaning is something we make and impose on the world.) Specifically, we have come to believe that meaning is something created in our brains and which we place onto a neutral, indifferent world. As buffered selves, it feels natural for us to conceive of meaning as a thing we determine inwardly. There is no inherent meaning in anything: nature, marriage, texts, feelings, experiences, and so on. But we can impose meaning on a naked universe by the force of our will. We can devise games, rituals, competitions, hermeneutics, and stories that give existence meaning.

One reason this generic existentialism is so popular is that it fits nicely with expressive individualism and instrumental reason, two of the strongest influences on our society. Both expressive individualism and instrumental reason rely primarily on the buffered self. In expressive individualism, we discover, create, or choose our identity inside of us and then express it in the world.

In instrumental reason, we use disengaged reason to internally interpret the world and then we impose that meaning on the world. The key here is that meaning exists inside of us. All we have to do is live authentically according to it.

WHERE WE LOOK FOR THE PATH TO FULLNESS

Part of the experience of living in the modern world is the sense that we have been thrown back on ourselves. We may not be living in an ordered cosmos that reveals the goodness and character and laws of God, and we might not have shared values and ideals any longer, but we do have our individualism and our interpretations of the world to ground us. As the external world grows increasingly fractured, hostile, and uncertain, the inner self, which is protected from these forces with the buffer of rationalism, gives us a way to determine meaning. The problem is that we are pressured by society to conform to its standards, and culture is so ingrained in us that it is hard for us to see our true self—to sort out what is really "me" and what is a foreign influence.

So the quest for authenticity has become a central narrative of the contemporary West. To be fully human, we must discover who we are, actualize our identity, express ourselves, be true to ourselves, and so on. Here again we see the influence of existentialism: to live authentically is to live faithfully to the meaning we discover, rather than to live in submission to external authorities. But is this quest achievable? Can we know our true self?

The quest for authenticity assumes that we will discover our authentic self if we will only turn inward, dig deep enough, face our monsters, and adequately express what we find. But before we get there, we need to ask the question, What is a self? Are we the combination of personality traits, skills, spiritual gifts, and intelligence that can be used to describe us? We tend to think so. In fact, there are entire industries built around the singular quest to know ourselves. Everything from horoscopes to personality tests to spiritual gift tests to IQ tests purport to peel back our masks, to dig beneath our fears, to reveal who we *really* are. And why do we want to know? So we can make choices consistent with who we are.

But no test can actually define the real you. Your personhood is irreducible to any list, which is why the scientific basis for most personality tests is weak. (One of the most popular tests, the Myers-Briggs Type Indicator, is notably unreliable.)[4] Personality tests are desperate attempts to quantify the unquantifiable, yet we are driven to them because when we can define and circumscribe something, we can gain some mastery over it. And the feeling of mastery over our self, even if it is based on flawed tests, is reassuring in a world of flux. Some of us even become obsessed with personality tests. We display them proudly online ("Husband, Father, Professor, Follower of Christ, ENTP. RT =/= endorsements"), refer to them in conversation ("But when she told me she was leaving, I really didn't get what the big deal was because I'm an INTJ, so 'feelings' are hard for me to interpret"), and make major life decisions on their basis ("George Washington was an ISTJ too? I guess I'd better lead a revolution").

But even if these tests *were* shown to be empirically reliable, they still wouldn't get at what we mean by a *self*. They may be helpful ways to reflect on our personality, but they can't reveal us. After all, a self is a being with a history and experiences. A self is in fact made up of so many different qualities that it is impossible to truly, thoroughly *know* ourselves.

The irreducibility of personhood does not mean that it is unimportant to know ourselves. In fact, John Calvin begins his *Institutes of the Christian Religion* by claiming that we cannot know God unless we know ourselves. He then claims that we also cannot know ourselves *truly* until we know God, because the knowledge of God's goodness reveals our greater need for him.[5] The self-knowledge that Calvin advocates is an awareness of our human condition: our need for God. The goal here is not to discover a self so it can be expressed and actualized, but so it can be made more Christlike. When we make the time for contemplation, for meditating on Scripture, for self-reflection, we invite the Holy Spirit to interpret us, to reorder our desires, to cut through our self-deception so we can be honest. In chapter four, we will briefly look at how this kind of contemplation must play an important role in cultivating a disruptive witness.

The contemporary quest for your "authentic self" assumes that we each have a specific, knowable, ideal identity deep within us. But this quest does not fit with what we know about our minds and experience. People dramatically change over time. Our minds are highly malleable. What seems most true to who we are may actually be what is most disordered—our strongest desires are sometimes the most immoral. This means that there is no static, ideal self hidden within that we are morally obligated to discover and express to give our lives meaning and justification. In fact, the quest for the authentic self can cause great harm. We may discover what we want to discover. In this way, we find the "best" of ourselves, or the self that most supports our desires, which is the exact opposite of the kind of self-knowledge that Calvin says we need in order to know God. Alternatively, we may drive ourselves mad searching for something that never existed in the first place. And we move from one identity and passion to the next, trying desperately to find the meaning that will make us complete and whole. Sometimes this looks like jumping from career to career until the perfect fit is found. Other times the person goes from relationship to relationship until they find the person who completes them. But always, we lack true freedom.

The modern quest for authenticity assumes that once we find this self, we will have a basis from which to navigate the treacherous, shifting modern world. But we were made to live in community, and any atomistic basis for living will necessarily be incompatible with human flourishing. If my foundation for knowing my place, purpose, and end in this world is on the basis of a self-discovered hidden identity that only I can verify and properly know, and that others are obligated to accept by virtue of being outside of me and therefore are unable to judge, there is less space for collective human flourishing. There are only self-defining atoms, asserting their identity on the world through their will. Of course it is possible to discover a self that is committed to the common good, or a self that accepts external authority, but this quest has a natural bent toward narcissism.[6]

HOW FULLNESS MANIFESTS

Regardless of whether or not the quest for authenticity is achievable or sensible, most of us have adopted some version of it, and that means that there are potentially as many visions of fullness as there are individuals. If the good life looks like discovering and expressing yourself, then there is no shared good life, and it is hard to make a compelling argument that one individual vision of fullness is any better than another. Let's consider the case of two very different visions of fullness based on the inner self.

Is there a qualitative difference between a boy who discovers in himself a love of classical music and devotes his life to the study and performance of the classical piano and someone who chooses to identify as a vampire and devotes her life to acting out this identity? Let's work through some reasonable answers to this.

1. "Classical music is a rich, complex, beautiful, noble subject worthy of devoting one's life to. Vampirism is a silly game."

   This statement is only persuasive if we assume that upper-middle-class aesthetics are the ultimate judge of what is meaningful in life. Sure, vampirism isn't as culturally respectable, but if they both feel fulfilled, why does that matter?

2. "The boy who studied music lived an authentic life because he pursued what he was passionate about. Vampirism is entirely contrived."

   This raises the question, What was the boy really being authentic *to*? Was there some ideal musician stamped somewhere deep inside of him which he discovered and actualized? If so, where did the ideal come from? Isn't the very idea of becoming a professional classical musician entirely a social construct, just like vampirism? This too seems to be a poor foundation for differentiating visions of fullness.

3. "Classical music can be profitable and useful. It can help other people, and it contributes to society. Vampirism is only beneficial to those who play along with the fantasy."

This is persuasive only if you believe that one of the highest goods in life is serving your neighbor. If, on the other hand, the highest good is to live authentically according to who you are, there's no meaningful distinction here.

4. "Classical music has a tradition, institutions, texts, and a community to give the boy a sense of belonging to a story larger than himself. Vampirism is hardly even a thing."

Although it is not as widely known, modern vampires have their own organizations, texts, rituals, and communities through the miracle of the internet.

These two disparate visions of fullness demonstrate that appeals to the authentic self necessarily appeal to some other good besides the authentic self, whether it's middle-class aesthetics, altruism, utility, tradition, or something else. As Taylor notes,

> Our normal understanding of self-realization presupposes that some things are important beyond the self, that there are some goods or purposes the furthering of which has significance for us and which hence can provide the significance a fulfilling life needs. A total and fully consistent subjectivism would tend towards emptiness: nothing would count as a fulfilment in a world in which literally nothing was important but self-fulfilment.[7]

Because these higher goods go internally unacknowledged and publicly unarticulated, there is little we can say that separates these two visions of fullness except that one is historically and culturally praised as noble while the other is seen as silly and lame. We are left with two different narratives that give meaning and justification to two people. What tends to unite modern images of fullness like these is an acceptance of expressive individualism. The highest publicly acknowledged good is to be yourself fully, which you can only do by looking inward to discover your true self and then by expressing that self. That expression typically takes the form of narrative.

When we frame our life as a story, we imbue it with certain qualities that are inherent in that medium. Stories have an arc and a trajectory, just as we feel we must be moving toward some vision of the ultimate good "because we cannot but orient ourselves to the good, and thus determine our place relative to it and hence determine the direction of our lives, we must inescapably understand our lives in narrative form, as a 'quest.'"[8] Stories have a protagonist, just as our lives appear to have a central character: ourselves. They can also be coherently interpreted, whether they are stories of great pianists or vampires. Even avant-garde stories that deconstruct traditional narratives can be coherent in their tragic or ironic deconstruction. This is simply what stories do: they lift the subject out of the ordinary and onto a higher plane. If we tell the story of someone working a mundane job for thirty years, we will raise that person up as significant simply by virtue of telling their story, because stories draw our attention, our focus, our gaze to someone else in the world. Despite any postmodern efforts to deconstruct meaning in stories, when we approach a text, we anticipate meaning: This story will mean something, I will be able to interpret it, and it will have a definite, meaningful end. Of course, these are the same things we want to say about our own lives. And this gets at the vast differences in how people find meaning in their lives in 2018, something Charles Taylor calls "the nova effect."[9]

It's hard for us to grasp the nova effect, which Taylor describes as the tremendous explosion in ways people find meaning and justification in life. As Christianity has ceased to offer the vision of fullness shared by the vast majority of people in the West, in its place we find billions of micronarratives of fullness. We need all these stories to make sense of things, so it's no coincidence that humanity has never been more inundated with narratives than we are today. We are so oversaturated with stories that entire careers are devoted to helping others figure out which stories are worth our time, from the data scientists engineering Netflix's recommendation algorithm to popular YouTube video-game critics. Commercials are short narratives. Songs tell stories, as do movies, TV shows, social media postings, YouTube stars, and video games. Our stories are more pervasive, more diverse, and more immersive than ever. What these stories give us are ways of imagining meaning and justification in life—fullness.

Sometimes these visions of fullness are patently absurd: Coke commercials promising people a worry-free life, body spray that promises to attract beautiful women, a luxury car that promises a sense of stoic confidence in your power and importance in the world. But we are in on the joke. Rationally we know that none of these products will give us the fulfillment they advertise, but even so, their aesthetics still form us. So we might not really believe that the body spray will win us attractive women, but we feel a little more convinced that existential justification looks like being desired by beautiful women, especially when we are given the same vision of fullness in TV shows, on social media, and in other stories.

Other times, the visions of fullness we see in narratives are compelling. They present, not a rational case for how to have a meaningful and justified life, but an embodied, aesthetic argument that may include appeals to reason. And this is why stories are so important, because they don't just make a claim like "Living a life of service to the poor gives you meaning and value." They show that life. A good story will evoke the visceral experience of living toward a particular ideal of fulfillment.

As an example, Americans who watch an average amount of TV and film, and listen to modern music, will probably find it incredibly difficult *not* to believe that their lives can be justified if they find and marry the right person. Ernest Becker argues that the modern relationship is all many of us have left after the so-called "death of God."[10] When another human being looks directly into your eyes and confesses their self-giving love to you for life, that is a profound affirmation of your existence. In the church, we believe that marriage reflects something of the relationship with Christ and his church, and so we have a way of explaining why marriage feels so validating: it is an echo of Christ's justification of his church, his body. But it is only an echo, because unlike Christ, "No human relationship can bear the burden of godhood, and the attempt has to take its toll in some way on both parties."[11] If you look to any other person to give your life justification and meaning, you will eventually resent them and leave disillusioned. Yet this myth, this vision of fullness, continues to be one of the most enduring in the West. And we have seen this myth repeated in a million stories, so that no matter how many times we personally experience its emptiness, we still find it alluring.

While expressive individualism is the basis for most visions of fullness, the details of visions can be radically different, as we saw in the cases of pursuing classical music and vampirism. It is difficult for us to grasp the diversity of stories that give people meaning today. With the growth of the internet and globalization, it is possible for people to identify with incredibly exotic communities and lifestyles, giving their life drama, ethos, aesthetics, language, narrative, meaning, and justification.

I'm not describing hobbies here. These are immersive communities of shared meaning: organic living, dispensationalist Christian homeschooling, political activism, Renaissance Fair goers, anime cosplay, *World of Warcraft*, street-car racing, street preaching, DIY home renovation, professional video gaming, podcasting, 4chan, YouTube stars, and on and on. This short list only barely touches on some of the more mainstream of these visions of fullness. It doesn't begin to cover the visions of fullness that involve people identifying as someone or something else: animals, reincarnated beings, mythical creatures, children, and the like. Or those who find their meaning in some form of witchcraft, conspiracy theories, belief in aliens, or American, commercialized Eastern mysticism. The extreme examples of this are easy to spot and mock. You find them in British tabloids every few weeks: stories of people who have decided to live as dogs or babies, or who have gone through endless body modifications to appear as a lizard. But do not think of these immersive lifestyles as merely a thing weird people do; this is what most of us do today. Many hipsters, Silicon Valley techies, NASCAR enthusiasts, corporate-ladder climbers, online political activists, evangelical discernment bloggers, and English professors share a sense that their lives are granted meaning through their lifestyle. Whatever you are into, you can find a community to join, products to buy to shape your immediate surroundings to fit that lifestyle, a standard of excellence to work toward (a telos!), and activities to keep you distracted.

The flattening of belief in the modern world diminishes the distinction between a lifestyle and a belief system. If your extreme sports lifestyle determines your purpose, your sense of worth, your consumer choices, your ethics, and your aesthetics, it ceases to function as only a hobby or preference. It is your vision of fullness, at least until something new or more interesting comes along. And what's so wrong with that if it makes you happy and keeps you out of trouble and you remain a productive member of society and a healthy consumer?

The answer is, it probably doesn't make you happy, or at least, not for long, because you are always aware of other ways of interpreting the world, other meanings advocated by your neighbors. Charles Taylor identifies this fear as a part of the "malaise of immanence," a term he coined to describe the cluster of anxieties that are produced by a secular society: "A crucial feature of the malaise of immanence is the sense that all these answers are fragile, or uncertain; that a moment may come, where we no longer feel that our chosen path is compelling, or cannot justify it to ourselves or others. There is a fragility of meaning."[12] I don't believe that Taylor means to imply that all modern secular people suffer under this anxiety. As I've already argued, I think our culture is impressively designed to keep us from the kind of self-reflection needed to identify, interpret, and resolve such an anxiety of meaning. But it is also true that the vast majority of modern people in the West have some sense of what the malaise of immanence feels like. And the question we all have is, What else is there?

CONTINGENT VISIONS OF FULLNESS

In a distracted, secular age, belief is fragile, fragmented, and thin. But we can try to cobble together a satisfying life of meaning and existential justification by pulling imagery from the endless narratives that surround us. The vision of fullness we follow may not be coherent or robust enough to explain the richness of existence, but whatever it is lacking can be filled in with other beliefs or simply ignored.

For Christians, there are three major takeaways from this account of how we find meaning and justification in the contemporary world. First, we have an obligation to examine ourselves and see how we may unknowingly find our meaning and justification in one of the billion micronarratives that fill our culture. In fact, I would venture to say that most of us have already adopted parts of these secular visions of fullness. To take the most personally convicting example, many of us who profess faith in

Christ actually find most of our existential justification in romance or career success or intelligence or beauty or popularity, and we find our meaning in a secular telos of achievement. If we try to bear witness to Christ's finished work on the cross, but in practice we have set our eyes on some secular vision of fullness, our faith will be perceived as just another consumer preference, something we can add to our current lifestyle.

Second, our response to a distracted, secular age cannot be a retreat into authentic individualism as it is commonly understood. The quest for the platonic form of yourself deep inside you leads to self-deception, autonomous creation, or despair. Christians should be reflective and contemplative, which we will explore in the second part of this book, but our reflection is not a kind of mystical hunt for our true self, deep within. Our personhood is revealed in part through knowing ourselves and our sin. If the world feels phony and thin, the answer is not a more rigorous turn inward to find the ground of being, but a turn outward toward God.

Third, to bear witness to our faith we need to be attuned to how our neighbors conceive of meaning and justification, what visions of fullness move them, and where they have found particular visions wanting. The desire to live a life of meaning and to have our being in the world justified is natural and good, but our goal is not to offer them just another vision of fullness to add to their options. A disruptive witness denies the entire contemporary project of treating faith as a preference.

PART TWO

BEARING A DISRUPTIVE WITNESS

4

DISRUPTIVE PERSONAL HABITS

The description of our distracted, secular age that I have developed over the first three chapters of this book might give the impression that there's little hope. How can we reasonably expect to alter our society so that our neighbors are primed to receive the gospel as a radical, irreducible truth? I think that's a fair question. The problem *is* too big. It is a deeply embedded cultural condition, supported by a multitude of practices, institutions, and values that need to be uprooted in some cases and reclaimed in others.

Our habit of distraction is built into our technology, our jobs, and our social lives. We can try to resist it in our own lives and in our spheres of influence—but what about the rest of society? Similarly, we have seen how, for most contemporary people, secularism is not a cognitive rejection of religion, but a subtle and deeply ingrained cultural assumption, one with serious implications for how we view and identify ourselves. We can call people's attention to the assumptions of secularism and the conceptions of the self that frame our understanding of the good life and the Christian faith, but practically, no amount of raising awareness can undo the influence of an entire culture undergirded by secularism.

If history is any indication, the distracted, secular age can only be uprooted by a tremendous historical event that reorders society, technology, and our entire conception of ourselves as individuals: something like the invention of the printing press, the Protestant Reformation, or a global war—a paradigm-shifting event. But trying to correct the effects of secularism and distraction through some massive event is quixotic at best and mad scientist-ish at worst. This leaves us in a difficult position. There is no reasonable, society-wide solution.

Which is not to say that we can't ameliorate the problem through policies and community practices. Collectively, we could put pressure on app developers and smartphone designers to stop making distraction a central goal of their design, an effort currently being led by the advocacy group Time Well Spent.[1] Primary schools could move away from screens as much as possible and extend reading and silent-reading times. Christians could pressure companies to use ethical marketing that does not rely on selling us a vision of the good life with our dish soap. In politics, we could insist that religion is not an irrational corrupter of civil public discourse but instead a legitimate member of society that deserves a seat at the table. In his book *The World Beyond Your Head: On Becoming an Individual in an Age of Distraction*, Matthew B. Crawford argues that there needs to be greater respect for what he calls the "attentional commons," our shared resource of attention.[2] Crawford makes several practical recommendations to preserve the attentional commons, like requesting that shopping malls not have speakers "in every single corner of the shopping mall."[3] Like Crawford, I would encourage those in positions of influence to make decisions that nudge people toward contemplation. It may be that whatever changes come in the near future will somehow return us to a more contemplative culture that acknowledges the transcendent as valid and good—but I have my doubts. By themselves, the results of any one of these policies would be valuable but still inadequate to effect substantive change to our society's condition.

We simply can't reorder society or argue our way out of this societal condition. We are here and we should expect little to change—except perhaps an even greater dependence on radical individualism and distraction among the middle and upper classes as technology continues to evolve. And yet, despite the intransigence of the problem, inaction is also unacceptable. It is not an option for us to accept these cultural changes and their ramifications and continue on as the church has in America for the last one hundred years. To some extent, the church in America has been shielded from the more persuasive criticisms against it by its lingering support for evangelical ethics and lifestyle. But that is quickly evaporating. I fear that by unknowingly accepting some of the premises of secularism (for example, presenting Christianity as the best lifestyle option) and uncritically embracing the technology of distraction, the American church will be unable to effectively compete in a marketplace of ideas in which Christian sexual ethics and traditional teachings are increasingly viewed as repugnant. Only a Christianity that is *more* than just another option on the market can retain its voice when its ethics become culturally offensive.

As I shift from describing our current condition to prescribing some ways of cultivating a disruptive witness, we need to take an honest look at the likelihood that we can make a difference on a societal level. The second half of this book does not aim to solve the problems of secularism and technology-driven distraction, but it does offer concrete, achievable, meaningful actions to help the church preserve its witness.

The best strategy for addressing our society's condition is to offer a disruptive witness at every level of life. On the personal level, we need to cultivate habits of contemplation and presence that help us accept the wonder and grandeur of existence and examine our assumptions about meaning and transcendence. At the level of the church, we must abandon practices adopted from the secular marketplace that trivialize our faith, and instead return to traditional church practices that encourage contemplation and awe before a transcendent God. Finally, in our cultural participation, we can reveal the cross pressures of the secular age and create space for conversations about the kind of anxieties and delights that we repress in order to move through adulthood. The order of these levels in the following chapters does not reflect a priority or chronology. The church's liturgy, for example, does not come after we form personal habits. Rather, the personal, liturgical (in the sense of church liturgy), and cultural each overlap and affect one another.

At each level, our expectation is not to undo hundreds of years of deeply ingrained secular ideas and the more recent forces of distraction that exacerbate them, but to offer an earnest, principled resistance to forces in our culture that are harmful to human flourishing and create barriers to the gospel. Specifically, we need to stop adopting practices and language that contribute to the trivializing of the Christian faith, reframe our vision so God is the end we pursue, not ourselves, and advocate for policies and practices that encourage honest contemplation and help our neighbors limit the force of the buffered self.

REORIENTING OUR MOVEMENTS

The heart of our distracted, secular age is a cognitive movement toward the individual. This does not mean that we no longer care about the welfare of our neighbor because we are so absorbed with ourselves. On the contrary, as Taylor notes, a kind of "horizontal transcendence," a focus on beneficent humanism, has taken the place of vertical transcendence for many modern people. People seek fulfillment in the endless work of ending suffering. Instead, the movement I am describing has to do with the attentional and perspectival focus on the individual. Everything in culture seems to be addressed *to us*, calling to us for attention, resources, money, value, and approval, from ads to devices to politicians. And as buffered selves, we experience a great degree of focus on our individual perspective and choices. (It's worth considering to what extent the buffered self may be in part a *defense* against the overwhelming and unending calls for our attention we experience daily.)

Safe within our heads, we interpret what is good, what is true, what is beautiful, and who we are. We do this not because we are narcissistic (although we may be) but because this is our default way of being in the world. Based on my experience, my head is *the* subject of existence. David Foster Wallace famously described this background belief: "Everything in my own immediate experience supports my deep belief that I am the absolute center of the universe, the realest, most vivid and important person in existence."[4] Although Wallace refers to this basic belief as "hard-wired," I think a more historically informed take is that while we naturally perceive the world through our own experiences, the sense that we are the absolute center of the universe was much more difficult to believe in the 1400s, when the universe was seen as a cosmos with God at the center. The temptation is to believe that the way we experience life today is fundamentally the same as someone six hundred years ago except for our material conditions, but the image of ourselves as the authoritative interpreters and protagonists in the story of existence is a fundamentally modern construct.

This construct involves a movement we need to challenge if we are to address a distracted, secular age. All things are moving toward an endpoint in our head. We conceive of our lives as the journey of our consciousness over time. We interpret experience to give meaning to our lives. And even when we act selflessly, our attention is drawn to how that selfless act develops our identity and the narrative of our lives—how it makes us look or feel or behave. Existence is directed toward ourselves.[5] Bearing a disruptive witness involves adopting a new movement, a shift in ends from ourselves to a transcendent God, and then letting that shift shape us in every aspect of our lives.

I chose the word *movement* because it captures the sense of flow involved in *reorienting* ourselves toward God. This isn't a change in belief about God. If you are an orthodox Christian, you already believe in the God of the Bible who transcends and sustains all creation and yet chose to enter into creation in the form of a man, and who indwells creation in the church, which is his body here on earth. By *movement* I mean a habit of exercising belief that can form our hearts to know God.[6] The result of these habits should be a deeper sense that we live in a created world sustained by a loving God, and an openness to the way creation and revelation pierce our buffered selves and interpret us.

Allow me a somewhat peculiar illustration to help us comprehend this movement. Envision a long mountain river leading into an expansive lake. People come from hundreds of miles to swim, boat, fish, and play in and on the lake, which makes the lake rather vain. The lake imagines itself to be the ultimate destination for the river. As far as the lake is concerned, the river's purpose is to fill it up, and from that water the lake becomes a place of meaning, value, and fullness. And to the lake, the river seems to be self-sustaining. Water just naturally comes from it. But unbeknownst to the lake, the river has a source behind it: the rain clouds. And those clouds don't just send the rain that falls on the mountains and flows down to the lake; they sustain other lakes, animals, and vegetation, as well as the people who come to play on the lake. Everything good comes down from on high as a gift, and without the clouds, everything in the lake's world would cease to be.

Now suppose someone were to talk to the lake. Perhaps one day the river whispers to its neighbor, "You know, I didn't make myself. This water comes from the snowpack in the mountains, and that comes from the clouds. And the water flows down all over the mountains, not just to you." If the lake could get past its wounded ego and recognize the river as a gift from the clouds, it would be overwhelmed with gratitude and look upward to the sky—a movement back to the clouds and an acknowledgement of its contingency on the clouds. And so the lake evaporates a bit each day, without ceasing. Just as the river flows into the lake, the lake also looks up to the sky so that it never again sees itself as the end of the river, but always as the grateful recipient of grace from the clouds.

My illustration breaks down, however, because the water cycle is self-sustaining. The clouds require evaporation in order to form and produce rain. Each part of the cycle requires the others. But the glory we give to God for his provision does not sustain him in the least, and he does not need to provide for us in order to receive glory. Both his love for us and our love for him are motivated not by necessity but by gratuitous love, which ought to make our desire to glorify him all the greater.

This is the movement we need—a *double movement* in which the goodness of being produces gratitude in us that glorifies and acknowledges a loving, transcendent, good, and beautiful God. Simply put, the double movement is the practice of first acknowledging goodness, beauty, and blessing wherever we encounter them in life, and then turning that goodness outward to glorify God and love our neighbor. Such a practice challenges the secular assumption of a closed, materialist universe. It shifts our focus away from expressing our identity and toward glorifying God, and it lifts our attention to a telos beyond ourselves and our immediate entertainment.

THE DOUBLE MOVEMENT IN SCRIPTURE

Growing up in the church, I was regularly taught that we need to "put Christ on the throne of our lives." I distinctly remember a visual used in church to show the two choices in life: either we are on the throne of our life or God is. To be saved is to submit to the Lord, to accept him as Lord over every part of our life. In some ways, this was tied to the idea of worldview, and to another visual: becoming Christian means putting on a pair of "Christ glasses," which help us see the world truly for the first time. Both visuals emphasized the authority of Christ over the realm of morality. If God is on the throne of my life, then I have to obey him and not lie. If I put on my Christ glasses, I cannot see porn as harmless; it is sinful and destructive. And of course, both of these ideas are true: Christ *is* Lord over me, and believing in him *does* change the way I interpret the world. But as true as these images are, they don't go far enough to address the influence of secularism.

It is not hard to accept Christ as a moral authority and Christianity as a lifestyle without ever *really* believing that Christ, the Son of God, came to earth as a man and died on the cross for our sins and is interceding for us now before the throne of God. Faith can be a lifestyle choice, even if we avidly believe it's the best lifestyle choice and everyone else is totally missing out by not getting on board with us. Again, the temptation for evangelicals today is to identify as Christians while functionally living like the scoffers Peter warns us about: "Where is the promise of his coming? For ever since the fathers fell asleep, all things are continuing as they were from the beginning of creation" (2 Peter 3:4). The slow march of mechanical time in a closed, impersonal universe is the overwhelming sense of existence given to us by modernity. And in such a world, Christ's lordship must extend beyond our morality. It must seep into our bones and affect the way we live and move in the world *as* a work of divine creation. And for that, we need a habitual movement toward God.

We find a model for this double movement throughout Scripture, but perhaps the most vivid example is during the Sermon on the Mount when Christ exhorts us: "Let your light shine before others, so that they may see your good works and give glory to your Father who is in heaven" (Matthew 5:16). This verse has always bothered me because my impulse is not to let others see my good works. First, I feel like a fraud who has never really done anything good. Second, even if I have done something good, I don't want to draw attention to it. Yet Christ commands me to let my light shine. Notice the double movement here. Others see something good, but their love and admiration for that good work does not *end* with the work. It moves upward to glorify God.

This is the proper movement whenever we encounter anything good in life. We acknowledge its goodness and we give glory to God. This is the antithesis of the reaction of the scoffers Peter mentions, who look out into the world (which God called "good") and mock the idea of his existence. I suspect if we were able to speak to these scoffers, they would readily admit that there is good in creation. There is beauty, pleasure, delight, and wonder, but it primarily resides in their heads. They see a sunset and judge it beautiful. Their individual perception and appreciation of goodness is the end of goodness because there is no one to be grateful *to*—although they may have a sense of pride in their ability to judge the sunset. And that is what mostly replaces gratitude for creation in the contemporary world: an overweening pride in the human ability to perceive, define, circumscribe, discover, measure, test, validate, reproduce, analyze, categorize, or otherwise contain the universe.

Paul takes up this double movement in 1 Corinthians 10:31, when he tells the church in Corinth, "Whether you eat or drink, or whatever you do, do all to the glory of God." If you allow these words to settle in, Paul's command is overwhelming. There is no space left for us to act for our own glory. We can't just act *morally* to the glory of God. Every action ought to have its telos in God and his glorification. Paul's words imply a constant state of glorification of God, which calls to mind his exhortation in 1 Thessalonians 5:17 to "pray without ceasing." The image of Christian life presented by Paul is one in which an awareness of God's presence is constant, and nothing good, beautiful, or true ends with us. There is always a movement to God.

The double movement I've been describing is not merely a cognitive affirmation of God's existence. It ought to necessarily shape our actions as well. This could begin with something simple, like the decision to pause for a moment when we encounter something beautiful so that we can momentarily contemplate its beauty and say a prayer of thanks. For example, when I was younger and I saw an attractive woman, I had a few responses. I would lust, I would look away from her to avoid the temptation, or I might feel a kind of bitterness, knowing that her beauty was not mine to enjoy and never would be. In each case, the terminus of my experience of her beauty was my head, and the responses were usually unloving to the woman and dishonoring to God. And it made me miserable. Then I adopted a prayer: "Dear God, thank you for her beauty and that it is not mine to participate in." The double movement of this prayer allows me to rightly appreciate beauty, give God the glory for his creation, affirm the goodness of her beauty, and decenter myself in the experience of beauty.[7] Practices like saying grace for meals and taking a sabbath rest can also form our social imagination in this way. As we will see in chapter five, church liturgy can also help us develop these practices.

LIVING ALLUSIVELY

When we practice this double movement to God in every area of our lives, it grounds our experience of the world in the fact of its createdness and God's prodigality, both of which work against the predominant sense that we live in a material world controlled exclusively by physical laws and human ingenuity. One place we see this is in aesthetics, the standards or theory of beauty. Typically, aesthetics is thought of as a subject for artists, poets, and philosophers, but evaluating and enjoying beauty is actually a fundamental experience of being human. We make aesthetic judgments every day, whether we're evaluating a song or deciding what to wear. Although we may not think of these as aesthetic judgments, that's what they are. Calvin Seerveld, a Reformed aesthetician, argues that Christians are called to live *aesthetic lives*. For those of us without artistic inclinations, such a calling may sound like yet another burden to add to our list of obligations for righteous living, but Seerveld's prescription is not a burden but a delight, and one that has disruptive potential.

In his book *Rainbows for the Fallen World*, Seerveld makes the case that all Christians are called to live an aesthetic life, and that at the heart of aesthetics is "allusiveness." "Aesthetic life," he writes, "is that kind of human activity which is peculiarly and principally responsive to God's creational ordinance of allusiveness, which holds somehow for all creaturely reality."[8] An allusion is a reference, a hint, a sign pointing toward something else. Seerveld believes allusiveness is a "creational ordinance" because it is the nature of creation to allude to God. Everything we see, experience, feel, hear, taste, touch alludes to some other part of the universe, which all ultimately allude to the Creator. Good art intentionally weaves in allusions not only to other works (which is the traditional way we think of allusion), but also to truths about the existence and nature of God.

> We western Christians, impregnated by hundreds of years of influential humanism, are also wont to think more highly of ourselves and our human technological achievements than we ought to think. It puts us in our place to realize every creature is made to praise God. All things are transparent manifestations of his power and wisdom. It is the very nature of creation that the whole world is like a burning bush— even though we walk around all the time with our shoes on. This is why the Old Testament singers sang about loving the

law of God (Psalm 119), taking delight in the provident order that graciously surrounds, structures and buoys up every living thing, even shining through the lowly stones.[9]

The key to delighting in beauty is the double movement. First we recognize the thing of beauty, then our minds are drawn onward and upward toward God. What makes a work of art, a poem, or a flower beautiful is the way it suggests more, the way it opens up possibilities, the way it alludes to other things in creation. In no way does this diminish the beauty of an object. It shows that its beauty is performed in its relation to other pieces of creation.[10]

In this way, the experience of reading a good novel or watching a good film is a receding horizon of allusions, evoked one after another or all at once, always onward and upward, always hinting more, always inexhaustible precisely because God is inexhaustible. Aesthetics reveals an irreducible universe—a universe that resists all our attempts at totalizing and controlling it, that is always just out of grasp, that always offers us a little more meaning. Yet it does all this without slipping into a kind of hyperreality of postmodernism. Allusiveness has a referent—a source—and yet that referent always involves more, because in the final account all allusions point back to the Creator and Sustainer of heaven and earth. A postmodern understanding of allusion, however, would posit that allusions have no ultimate referent. They began nowhere in particular and end nowhere in particular. This conception of the infinite is referred to by some contemporary theorists as the "sublime." Rather than a transcendent presence that allusions point to, the sublime is the absence of meaning and being at the center of all allusions.[11]

Understood like this, allusiveness is an experiential reminder that the material world is not complete, that a secular account of our being leaves us wanting and cannot meaningfully explain the richness of our lives. Seerveld says that "if the aesthetic moment is missing in daily active responses to God and neighbor in the world, then that life is shorn of a great praise potential and you are liable to a closed down kind of grim slavery, void of response to the calling of allusiveness."[12] Living aesthetically is disruptive because it unsettles the artificial *naturalness* of living in a closed, materialist world.

Let me use a brief example from literature to illustrate how an allusive novel can work to gesture toward a transcendent God. Many literary critics consider Cormac McCarthy's *Blood Meridian* to be one of the most important novels of the second half of the twentieth century. If you know anything about this novel, it may seem strange indeed that I would choose it for this task. *Blood Meridian* is a masterpiece, but it is also extremely violent and hopeless. It is the story of a band of former Civil War soldiers who go to Mexico to hunt for Apache scalps for the Mexican government. After slaughtering Apaches for profit, the band realizes that the scalps of peaceful natives look the same as scalps of Apaches, so they begin killing them as well. Eventually the Mexican government sends their army to stop the mercenaries. The novel includes horrifying accounts of massacres, sexual assault, and child abuse.

But a presence haunts the text. Throughout the novel are allusions to God's existence: ruined churches, an ex-priest, discussions about the existence of God, a baptism, a Bible, prayer. In a world utterly devoid of justice, the reader yearns for some being capable of bringing order, some source of goodness by which we could condemn the violence with confidence. At one point in the novel, the ex-priest tells the protagonist that God's voice is like horses grazing at night: we only notice his voice when he stops talking. When the horses stop grazing, we realize that they had been grazing the entire time.[13] In *Blood Meridian* the apparent absence of justice (the "silence" of God) makes the characters and the reader yearn for God. Thus, even in works of art that seem nihilistic, there can be rich allusions that draw our minds toward the goodness of God. This novel, which only points to God allusively through the apparent absence of earthly justice, may do more to draw us to God than saccharine Christian paintings that try to explicitly describe God.[14] The former subtly disrupts us and our expectations about the world, while the latter only confirms and exploits the rigidly defined image of Christian culture as a marketing demographic.

I used an example of a novel to explain how allusiveness may function, but Seerveld's focus is not primarily with literature. In fact, Seerveld argues that we go astray when we make aesthetics the sole domain of art, rather than life in general. Living aesthetically can take many forms, but in each case the emphasis is on inspiring the imagination to speculate about the multiplicity and grandeur of God's creation, goodness, and love.

This may look like decorating your home with photographs that arrest your guests and draw them in. So many prints sold in chain stores are far from captivating or imaginative. They are forgettable because the composition and subject are something our minds barely recognize as notable and because we've seen the same sorts of images in other homes or in the store. Rather than buying mass-produced art prints, we can find a painting or photograph at a thrift store that reminds our guests of the inexplicability of life. Or better yet, we can find a local artist to support, or hang our own photographs or paintings. My point is that living aesthetically does not mean spending a lot of money or having "high culture" taste. High culture is as susceptible to adopting tedious, unimaginative home decor as middle- or lower-class culture. The allusiveness of our world is not a product of our wealth or status, and neither wealth nor status are required to reflect that allusiveness in our homes. All we need is imagination and the desire to make the double movement.

The effort to live aesthetically disrupts our secular vision of the world as it is processed and packaged in the marketplace (which promotes endless *stuff* but not endless *good*) by unsettling our notions of a containable universe and the self-defined individual. There is a gratuitous quality to living aesthetically; it defies pragmatism and utilitarianism, but also greed and envy. Aesthetic living is unnecessary for survival, but it's an appropriate goal because it reflects the gratuitous creation of the world by God. The universe itself is contingent on God for both its creation and continued being. So aesthetic living reminds us that there is always more out there, and that "always more" points definitely toward a particular God, not an absence. Done well, aesthetic living is not a burden or an obligation for those privileged with time and money. Because God created a beautiful and vast world, we don't need wealth or an inordinate amount of time to order our lives to reflect that majesty. We need only the will to acknowledge and live openly in this world.

AN INDIVIDUAL OR A PERSON?

The double movement may seem to leave no room for purely individual actions. If the terminus of everything we do is in God and his glory, is there any space left for the individual? The answer to this is related to the larger question of whether we are *individuals* or *persons*. The modern concept of the self, with its perspective of sovereignty and objectivity and its buffer against external powers, leads to individualism, which the French philosopher Emmanuel Mounier defines this way:

> Individualism is a system of morals, feelings, ideas and institutions in which individuals can be organized by their mutual isolation and defence. This was the ideology and the prevailing structure of Western bourgeois society in the 18th and 19th centuries. Man in the abstract, unattached to any natural community, the sovereign lord of a liberty unlimited and undirected; turning towards others with a primary mistrust, calculation and self-vindication.[15]

Individuals need an *identity* to define themselves against the crowd. And as we have seen, that identity is envisioned as an internal ideal that can be discovered if we know ourselves and act authentically. This is key: in individualism, the image of the individual is either chosen, discovered, or created through an inward process. The terminus of the search for identity is always inside the individual, although it may be influenced by external sources.

We can see how this is incompatible with the double movement. If we replace the *individual* with the *person*, however, we can see how the double movement enriches our personhood rather than robbing us of space for difference.

Christian personalism is a philosophical movement that started between the world wars, primarily in France. In his foundational text on the movement, Emmanuel Mounier differentiates personalism from individualism by noting that the latter is focused only on inwardness and defending the individual, whereas personalism moves inward only to move outward.

> The self-reflective movement which constitutes "the individual" contributes to the maintenance of the human shape. But the person is only growing so far as he is continually purifying himself from the individual within him. He cannot do this by force of self-attention, but on the contrary by making himself *available* . . . and thereby more transparent both to himself and to others. Things then happen as though the person, no longer "occupied with himself" or "full of himself," were becoming able— then and thus only—to be someone else and to enter into grace.[16]

To live a full life requires us to be self-reflective. Through reflection we can identify sins and errors, and uproot egotism, which Mounier describes as "purifying himself from the individual within him." But notice that the double movement is again at work: we turn inward only to turn outward toward others, and in communion with others we know ourselves.

In one's inner experience the person is a presence directed toward the world and other persons, mingled among them in universal space. Other persons do not limit it, they enable it to be and to grow. Thus the person only exists toward others, it only knows itself in knowing others, only finds itself in being known by them.[17]

We can be more specific than Mounier: we can say that in particular we find ourselves by being known by God, as well as other persons.[18] We look inward to know ourselves in relation to God. The terminus of our attention is not in ourselves but in God, which means that a personalist account of human being has plenty of space for a distinct person even while the person's ultimate identity finds its fullest expression only in God. Mounier's call to contemplation and self-reflection is a model of inwardness that challenges the modern conception of the self while also addressing the stultifying effects of a distracted age.

THE NEED FOR SILENCE

The forces of distraction and secularism intersect and perpetuate each other: we long for distraction in part because we are terrified of living in a meaningless world, and we struggle to discover a satisfying sense of fullness in the world because we are constantly distracted. In his *Pensées*, Blaise Pascal articulates the relationship between the frenetic distraction of the modern era and its spiritual crisis (even though the modern era meant 1670 for him).

From childhood on men are made responsible for the care of their honour, their property, their friend, and even of the property and honour of their friends; they are burdened with duties, language-training and exercises, and given to understand that they can never be happy unless their health, their honour, their fortune and those of their friends are in good shape, and that it needs only one thing to go wrong to make them unhappy. So they are given responsibilities and duties which harass them from the first moment of each day. You will say that it is an odd way to make them happy: what better means could one devise to make them unhappy? What could one do? You would only have to take away all their cares, and then they would see themselves and think about what they are, where they come from, and where they are going. That is why men cannot be too much occupied and distracted, and that is why, when they have been given so many things to do, if they have some time off they are advised to spend it on diversion and sport, and always to keep themselves fully occupied.[19]

Notice how similar this description is to the account of my daily life in chapter one, and then remember that Pascal wrote this in 1670. It's not clear to me whether this innate human desire to avoid reflection drove the technology of diversion or the other way around, but what is certain is that we have found a mutually beneficial arrangement: technology provides us distractions from ourselves, and we provide technology with attention. If this sounds a bit like the premise of *The Matrix*, don't get paranoid. The truth is probably less dramatic and more depressing: no evil, sentient computer or corporation is behind this. The human desire to hide from ourselves converged with the innovation of technology that aids that hiding, and the marketing of that technology is un-checked by questions of morality and the common good.

In Pascal's description of modern life, even relaxation becomes another kind of work, another thing to keep us busy. If we weren't diverted, we would be forced to explore fundamental life questions. In a later pensée, Pascal describes the effect this would have on us: "Take away their diversions and you will see them bored to extinction. Then they feel their nullity without recognizing it, for nothing could be more wretched than to be intolerably depressed as soon as one is reduced to introspection with no means of diversion."[20] Extinction, intolerable depression, and misery:

> The only thing that consoles us for our miseries is diversion. And yet it is the greatest of our miseries. For it is that above all which prevents us thinking about ourselves and leads us imperceptibly to destruction. But for that we should be bored, and boredom would drive us to seek some more solid means of escape, but diversion passes our time and brings us imperceptibly to our death.[21]

There is a destructive cycle to diversions. Like a drug addiction, diversions are both the cause of and a respite from what ails us. But Pascal offers a glimmer of hope: without distraction, "boredom would drive us to seek some more solid means of escape."

Although Christians, of all people, should not be afraid to be alone in the dark of the modern world, many of us rely on distractions to get us through the day. This can be true even when we devote ourselves to religious activities. Think about how easy it is to be busy but unmoved at church camp, for example. So long as we think of our faith as just a part of our identity, the trappings of Christian culture can be a perfect diversion. Ironically, by avoiding reflection we close ourselves off to the spiritual resources we need in order to survive modernity, as Pascal notes. The question is, What does healthy contemplation look like? How can we be self-reflective without falling into the abyss of self-absorption? What are we hoping to discover or accomplish by contemplation? And how can we create space for reflection in a distracted age? To answer these questions, we need to return to John Calvin's *Institutes*.

Like Pascal, Calvin believes that human flourishing involves honest self-reflection (the first movement) which reveals misery and leads us outward to God (the second movement). Calvin's description of the tension between the knowledge of God and self is so powerful it is worth quoting at length.

> Our wisdom, in so far as it ought to be deemed true and solid wisdom, consists almost entirely of two parts: the knowledge of God and of ourselves. But as these are connected together by many ties, it is not easy to determine which of the two precedes, and gives birth to the other. For, in the first place, no man can survey himself without forthwith turning his thoughts towards the God in whom he lives and moves; because it is perfectly obvious, that the endowments which we possess cannot possibly be from ourselves; nay, that our very being is nothing else than subsistence in God alone. In the second place, those blessings which unceasingly distil to us from heaven, are like streams

conducting us to the fountain. Here, again, the infinitude of good which resides in God becomes more apparent from our poverty. In particular, the miserable ruin into which the revolt of the first man has plunged us, compels us to turn our eyes upwards; not only that while hungry and famishing we may thence ask what we want, but being aroused by fear may learn humility. For as there exists in man something like a world of misery, and ever since we were stript of the divine attire our naked shame discloses an immense series of disgraceful properties, every man, being stung by the consciousness of his own unhappiness, in this way necessarily obtains at least some knowledge of God. Thus, our feeling of ignorance, vanity, want, weakness, in short, depravity and corruption, reminds us . . . that in the Lord, and none but He, dwell the true light of wisdom, solid virtue, exuberant goodness. We are accordingly urged by our own evil things to consider the good things of God; and, indeed, we cannot aspire to Him in earnest until we have begun to be displeased with ourselves. For what man is not disposed to rest in himself? Who, in fact, does not thus rest, so long as he is unknown to himself; that is, so long as he is contented with his own endowments, and unconscious or unmindful of his misery? *Every person, therefore, on coming to the knowledge of himself, is not only urged to seek God, but is also led as by the hand to find him.*[22]

Like the contemporary advocate for expressive individualism, Calvin calls us to turn inward so we can become more fully human—but this isn't a quest for an ideal image of our identity. What we find when we examine ourselves is not authoritative but *descriptive*.

With quiet reflection, our desires, fears, beliefs, doubts, and sins are given space to surface, but none of these define us. They may describe a part of our person at a particular moment in time, but only a part, and only for a time. If, however, we fail to make the double movement, then what we discover within us may appear to be definitive: "This is just who I am." The double movement draws us out of ourselves to a higher good. When we look inside and find abiding sin, the guilt of that sin takes us to the cross, where the One who took that guilt upon himself forgives us. When we look inside and find gratitude for a life we have been taking for granted (because diversions also rob us of our joy, as well as our misery), that gratitude draws us upward to God in thanksgiving. And when we look inside and reveal suppressed anxiety or dread, we can explore the source of that dread, knowing that the God who provides the peace that passes understanding loves us.[23] In contemplation, we know ourselves in relation to God, and as we grow in the knowledge of God, his truth interprets us, granting us deeper knowledge of ourselves. This is the "more solid means of escap[ing misery]" that Pascal hinted at—a God who reveals himself in us so we might know ourselves and in turn know him better.

Reflection like this requires regular, extended periods of time and attention, which for most of us probably feels impossible. I recommend that we begin with some low-hanging fruit. We are constantly distracted not just because there are so many interesting activities vying for our attention, but because we also cram in distractions between each of our activities. As I mentioned in chapter one, I struggle to walk upstairs without opening my phone to see what the latest news is. Calvin Seerveld described this condition and its causes in 1980, in what probably seems like a quaint passage today.

> As human time is geared to machine time to save time to give us "leisure," the pace of human life becomes inhuman. There is less and less slack time because the machines go so fast—conveyor belt-elevator-telephone-taxi vacuum cleaner-printing press—they begin to set the over-all tempo and *kind* of lickety-split, clickety-click kind of time, machine-time, for our lives. And if there should perchance be an instant break somewhere, an enterprising fellow is certain to fill it with something for somebody to "consume"—coin operated candy machine, billboard, jukebox, transistor radio.[24]

Oh, for the days when we only had to worry about enterprising fellows filling our time with candy machines and transistor radios! A practical, achievable step we can take toward reclaiming our attention and creating *some* space for reflection is to cut down on filler distractions. Make dinner without listening to a podcast. Use the bathroom without bringing your phone. Walk upstairs without checking Twitter, Alan. Stop seeing "unproductive" time as a problem to be solved and instead open yourself up to the possibility of undirected thought.

A habit like this can allow you to see God's creation anew, to process experiences, to reflect on sins, to be grateful. Most important, such a habit is an embodied claim that "redeeming the time" for the days are evil means redeeming it *for* God, for his glory, not for profitability, productivity, efficiency, or plain busyness. How on earth can we redeem each moment for him if we are so absorbed by the next thing that we forget he exists at all?

Another practical way to adopt a habit of reflection is to make prayer and meditation on the Word a daily activity. The disciplines of praying and reading the Bible center our attention outside of ourselves and on a conception of existence that transcends a material world. But the prayers of the buffered self profit little. We can easily turn these Christian disciplines into just another activity, if our time of prayer and meditation on the Word takes the posture of defense and closure to God's voice, conviction, and the Holy Spirit. None of us consciously do this, of course, but we do *unconsciously* approach the Holy Word of God and the throne of God without the fear and trembling and thankfulness that befit a people who believe that this book is divine revelation, and that our prayers rise up to a living God who loves us.

Consider: do you go to the Word and prayer with the unspoken sense that, as Peter says, "all things are continuing as they were from the beginning of creation"? Or do you believe in a risen King who is coming again in glory? If you struggle to believe, begin by thanking Christ for his love for you. Gratitude has a profound way of realigning our desires, and gratitude over a meal is a good place to start.

SAYING GRACE

I don't think I've ever felt comfortable saying grace before a meal, even at home, and when I'm in public I dread it. I try to time the prayer so that the server won't interrupt us. The idea of a server waiting while my family prays over a meal makes me feel self-conscious and guilty, as if I were imposing my religion on them. I don't want anyone around me to feel uncomfortable watching and listening to me pray. Besides, I tell myself, does it even matter if I pray for the food? I paid for it. I know I'm grateful. And I'm in a hurry. Isn't the necessity of saying grace just legalism—empty ritual that actually makes me *less* grateful? In the moment, especially when I'm hungry, it's much easier to start right in on the food and maybe, if I feel guilty, I can pray something silently like, "Sorry, God, but you know my heart."

It could be that you haven't experienced any reticence toward praying over a meal in public, but I hope you can see that many other Christians do feel uncomfortable. No small part of this discomfort stems from the rise of secularism in our country. Even in the fairly religious states I've lived in, such as Texas and Oklahoma, you don't see most people praying over their meals in public. Our society's broad assumption is that religious exercise belongs in our hearts, in our homes, or in our churches. It doesn't belong in a booth at McDonald's.

Public displays of religion are more offensive than public displays of affection, which I think partially explains some Americans' reactions to Muslims who say their daily prayers. For many Americans, seeing someone practicing religion in public feels a bit like watching the inebriated or mentally unstable in public: What are they going to do next? Why aren't they being rational? Why couldn't they keep this to themselves? Which is one reason why saying grace can be a testament to a watching world that our faith is not a personal preference that we keep discretely hidden behind our "normal" public life. And insofar as saying grace defies the secular social etiquette of privatizing religious practices, it is a disruptive witness.

We certainly shouldn't say grace in order to be seen saying grace, or to make people uncomfortable. We don't pray loudly so that others will be shocked and disturbed by our piety. Being a "Jesus freak" just to be a freak capitulates to the game of secularism in that it turns our faith into an advertisement, a signal to others. The practice of our faith turns out to be the advertising of our faith, which is the exact kind of hollowness at the core of so many contemporary beliefs we are seeking to avoid. If our public prayers or any other public display of faith ceases to be primarily about the spiritual purpose—in this case, thanking God for his provision—and instead becomes about others seeing us be thankful toward God, then we have exchanged the thing itself for the appearance of the thing. Our motive ought to be gratitude to God, not seeking attention. But if we find ourselves actually avoiding public prayers because it feels socially awkward, or because it feels like we're imposing our faith on our neighbors, we need to be able to call that avoidance what it is: a capitulation to secular ideas of the public square.

Another way that saying grace is a disruptive witness is that it challenges a materialist account of provision. Although there are nearly innumerable acceptable visions of fullness in our secular age, the majority of them assume that we live in a closed universe wherein everything or virtually everything can be explained through an empirical, materialist, scientific account. Physics and chemistry account for the totality of existence. We may come to many different conclusions from this assumption, however. For example, someone might look at the purely material world as a kind of nearly transcendent gift that requires our admiration and worship. Such a person may show gratitude for the idea of the Earth in all its vastness. Others may believe that the food in front of us is a testament to the human potential for greatness—our ability to cultivate the earth and produce fine food efficiently and economically. Still others may simply take provision as a given, not bothering to consider it at all except insofar as they are responsible for paying for the food.

What is uncommon is the view that whatever food lies before us is a gift from a personal God who provides for us because he loves us. The more divorced we are from the cultivation of crops and animals, and the more mechanical and manufactured our food appears to us, the less we see it as a gift. When our meals come to us carefully wrapped in paper from hands wrapped in latex gloves that took ingredients from hermetically sealed plastic bags that were created in a sanitary, automated factory, it is no easy thing to see the hand of God at work providing for us. Contingencies of weather and seasons, human errors, and animal behavior and health have been carefully, systematically, and technologically reduced as much as possible. Think, for example, of the fact that modern people *expect* to be able to go to the market and buy apples year-round. Humanity has mastered nature, and we owe humanity no gratitude—just some monetary compensation. This of course makes the act of giving thanks to God all the more disruptive. If I am thankful to the cook or the restaurant chain or capitalism or modern farming techniques or my job that allows me to afford the food or even a semimystical conception of Mother Earth, I am still fundamentally accepting that the food before me is completely the result of processes in the material world. But to thank God is to defy this logic. This is not a generic or impersonal sense of gratitude toward nature or the universe, but a specific thankfulness for a meal to a personal God whose common grace provides for us all.

Practiced regularly, saying grace is a reminder that the way things appear to us as modern people is not the truth of being. Underneath all the packaging and production and procedures remains God's providence and sustaining power. In truth, the world and our being within it is far more contingent than we know.

A SABBATH REST

The practice of resting on the sabbath is similarly disruptive. Even in my own Presbyterian tradition there is lively debate about what it means to keep the sabbath under the new covenant, whereas in the evangelical churches I grew up in, Sunday was just the day you went to church—unless you went to church on Saturday night, in which case Sunday was entirely indistinguishable from the rest of the week.

But there is a strong case to be made that an actual sabbath rest is important, in part because it best reflects our anthropology. We need rest and space for contemplation. Setting aside the sabbath for fellowship, rest, and acts of service deeply contradicts the standard way we understand the modern world. Thus it works to cut through the buffers we are inclined to erect as participants in modern culture, and presents a disruptive witness of the Christian faith.

Whether we keep the sabbath as a religious obligation or a spiritual discipline, it exists as a testament to the idea that humans do not define the movement of time. The sabbath is actually an imposition on our modern lives, in which we work fervently to flatten the distinction between all days. When no days are holy—set apart—then each day and each moment is raw material for us to do as we will. Time can come to be seen as the currency of our lives, and with whatever we purchase with that coinage, we define and redeem our existence. But the coinage itself remains neutral, unowed. Like so much else in the modern world, time becomes an instrument for our manipulation. We choose to give certain hours of our life to labor in exchange for payment, we live for the weekend, and we expend considerable resources on technology that can give us more free time or can help us fill dead time. In viewing time as raw material, we reject the idea that time may have meaning in itself, that it may be more than a measurement of intervals but contains truths that place obligations on us to act in certain ways.

But this was not always the case in Western society, and indeed is still not the case in many communities. Historically, the progression through the year, the month, the week, and the day were punctuated by holy times, sacred practices that defined the time for us, rather than our *choice* to participate being the defining act. Many in the Seventh-day Adventist communities still follow this, as do Eastern Orthodox, Catholic, Anglican, and Muslim communities. They recognize that certain days are spiritually set apart. The sabbath was made *for* humans, but this does not mean that the sabbath is made *by* humans. The difference is crucial. The practice of keeping the sabbath allows us to recognize that time has its own meaning. It is not an undifferentiated series of intervals.

A radically disruptive result of keeping the sabbath is that it denies the dominant cultural belief that we must always be working and doing. Particularly in an American culture that still suffers under the bastardization of the Puritan work ethic (which conflates righteousness with industriousness) and a sense that we are *always missing out on something important,* choosing to cease for one day every week is a disruptive witness to our neighbors. And it's an act of faith in God's providence—an embodied argument that fullness is not found in the desperate struggle of busyness. And yet it is hard for Christians to take a sabbath rest because Christianity can easily become yet another thing that fills our constantly busy life—something really no different from following football. There's always another event to do, another study to read, another program to attend, another way to catch up, get ahead, or try to get out of the hole. A sabbath rest is an act of spiritual defiance against the ideal of existential justification through production and consumption. It is a denial of the founding principle of the American Dream—that if you want to get ahead and reach the good life, you must always be working or self-improving.

A sabbath rest is a rest from our good works, even while it obligates us to works of service. The difference is that the rest is a rest in Christ's finished work on the cross. Sunday is not a day to "clean up our act" or "get right with God." It is a day to rest in our imputed righteousness by Christ and turn that joy outward (the double movement) into fellowship with our brothers and sisters, meeting together and sharing the table, ceasing from our labor, meditating on the Word and on God's natural revelation, and doing acts of service for our neighbors. I believe that sabbath rest also involves play—but it should be redemptive play, not the kind that consumes us and leaves us more mentally and emotionally drained than before. We should be refreshed, even if we are tired.

My recommendation is to see this time as a special time to love our neighbors. We might convene a small group on Sunday evenings or have people over for lunch or dinner. We should work hard throughout the week so we don't have to work on Sunday, but remember that there is grace for those moments when work must be done—the lost sheep must be found. It's wise to avoid shopping or work as a reminder that the marketplace is not the center of our lives, but a tool of culture we can use or abuse, like any other tool. We might also choose to rest from screens, or just smartphones and computers, and so create space for contemplation, reflection, and conversation. Alternatively, we might restrict our screen time to activities that are intentionally communal: watching a movie together, playing a game together, sharing photos and memories, or video chatting with family.

Thought of this way, the sabbath is a foreshadowing of the rest we have in Christ, which is not contingent on our good works. We don't need to work seven days a week to be valued and important, and we don't need to achieve spiritual maturity to receive God's grace. But it also foreshadows the end of this age, when we will rest from the curse of toil. And what a beautiful thing that will be! By resting and refusing to participate in the rat race, we act in faith that God will care for us and that this race is no path to salvation.

CONCLUSION

Adopting practices that push back against our distracted, secular age is a continual process, and it will take different forms for different people and different cultural contexts. What is important to take away from this is that we have agency. We are not merely the products of our culture. The Christian faith gives us resources to challenge distraction and secularism in our own lives, which naturally provides a disruptive witness to those around us. Making the double movement a habit can help us work against the pervasive sense that we live in a closed, immanent frame, while also calling us to a more mindful way of living. As we embody countercultural values and beliefs, we serve as lights in a world that many of our neighbors experience as dark, cold, and indifferent. But as valuable as these personal practices are, the greater witness must come from the church.

5

DISRUPTIVE CHURCH PRACTICES

The church can either define its witness by its worship, aesthetics, and rites or capitulate to secular conceptions of faith as a personal lifestyle preference. Each of us has an obligation to examine ourselves and the ways secularism and distraction have deceived us and left us seeking lesser, impoverished visions of fullness. As we work to embody our faith more richly in our personal habits, our lives can function as disruptive witnesses: signs to the watching world that life within the immanent frame does not require us to close off the transcendent, that there is a vision of fullness that doesn't require us to hide from silence, and that we are not trapped in a market of endless worldview choices. But as important as our personal efforts are, the greatest witness to the world will always be the body of Christ gathered to worship, which means that churches and denominations need to consider well what it means to bear witness in a distracted, secular age.

The church must embody the faith in such a way as to reveal its exclusivity, solemnity, transcendent power, incarnational theology, and authority. To accomplish this, we need to examine a host of practices, from how we read the Word during services to church signs and music. When our unbelieving neighbors see or visit our church, they should witness a spiritual gathering of saints worshiping a living and holy God.

They may feel uncomfortable or confused. They may feel embarrassed on our behalf for believing so sincerely in the efficacy of baptism and the Lord's Supper. But they also may find space to reflect on their misery—a space that invites and requests them to put aside distractions for a time. They may find an articulation of hope, beauty, love, and justice commensurate with their suppressed sense that these ideals are irreducible to any materialist explanation. But none of this can happen so long as our churches function merely as secular spaces for religious moralism and evangelical identity formation.

PLUGGING THE LEAKS

If the challenge of bearing witness in a distracted, secular age is that buffered people struggle to recognize the distinctiveness of the Christian faith, then our first task is to ensure that we are not inadvertently *helping* to obscure the gospel by adopting secular ideas that undermine it. Before bailing out a boat, it's best to plug the leaks. While we should apply this kind of self-reflection to every area of our lives, it is especially important to look at the ways we talk about, promote, frame, and discuss our faith. The way we describe our faith communicates the nature of our faith.

I have in mind here everything from church signs to Christian T-shirts to the setup of our church stages and pulpits. As the church has taken more and more of its cues from a secular, market-driven culture, we've picked up some bad habits and flawed thinking about branding, marketing, and promotion. We've tried to communicate the gospel with cultural tools that are used to promote preferences, not transcendent, exclusive truths.

In chapter one I used "Jesus Daily," allegedly the most active Facebook faith page in the world, as an example of what I called the trivializing tendency of the modern church. "Jesus Daily" takes poorly made images, adds some spiritual-sounding words, and goes viral. The owners of this page have simply taken the model of social media promotion used by other large viral-image pages to market their own brand. "Jesus Daily" might be an extreme example, but it's helpful because it demonstrates the kind of adaptation our churches can fall into. If that sounds ridiculous—if you think the trivialization I'm talking about isn't really an issue for you and your church—then withhold judgment for a few minutes and consider the following examples.

We see the same trends at work in high-production church services that feel more like a concert and TED Talk than a sacred event. High-quality video clips interrupt the sermon. The pastor paces the stage with a headset mic, skillfully weaving facts, stories, and dramatic pauses. The young, fashionably dressed worship band puts on a performance at center stage. The lighting and volume make it clear who the congregation should be paying attention to. Each element of the service alludes to bits of popular culture that draw the audience in. The cumulative effect is to give the impression that the Christian faith is something akin to a good motivational conference. It is personally useful and exciting and entertaining, but not disruptive in the least. On the contrary, it fits rather nicely with your current lifestyle.

To understand how this tendency can conflate Christianity with other lifestyle options, let's look at the example of T-shirts. Over time and with repetition, our minds associate stimuli with the ideas most often connected to them; so when we see or hear certain things we respond in certain ways. This may sound like a fault in our design, but it is actually a tremendously useful way for us to quickly navigate our sign-filled world. We need simple ways to categorize the kinds of information thrown at us hourly, so we make generalizations about messages based on the medium we receive them in. Graphic T-shirts, for example, are generally used to denote social or commercial affiliations: schools, teams, movies, bands, politics, favorite products. Often they are parodies or jokes. Some merely reflect a particular aesthetic sensibility. But almost without fail, a design on a T-shirt is meant to express to the world the choices you've made to define your identity. So when we wear Christian parody T-shirts or shirts with Scripture on them in hopes of sharing the gospel without having to speak to anyone, many of the people we run into will categorize our faith as just another personal preference, on par with political affiliation or music tastes.

The problem is not that we're expressing ourselves through our clothes: the reality is that we cannot *not* signal messages to people by what we wear. Since I took my first job as a professor, I've worn slacks, a dress shirt, and a tie almost exclusively. Part of my motive is that I enjoy wearing nice clothes, but I also want to signal to others (and to myself) that I'm a professional and that I take my job seriously. When I dress down to mow the lawn, my clothes signal to my neighbors that I'm doing some kind of manual labor. None of this is nefarious. Neither is it wrong for me to wear an Oklahoma City Thunder jersey—the Thunder are my favorite basketball team, and I like announcing that to the world as a show of solidarity with other fans. But choosing a sports team is actually quite trivial. When I use a T-shirt to try to communicate some spiritual truth, I am likely treating what is sacred as mundane. Even if I use a T-shirt to identify the church I attend, it's worth considering whether the branding will help people recognize and remember the church, or merely express another personal preference.

The example of T-shirts can be expanded to include a host of modern mediums: radio ads, fliers for a new sermon series, church architecture, bumper stickers, social media, video production, the pastor's language, the cover art on Christian music, book covers, billboards, religious paintings—the list goes on. There are no neat and tidy rules to determine whether or not a particular medium for bearing witness to our faith will instead undermine it by framing it as a cultural preference rather than a transcendent truth. We are in the realm of signs and interpretation; the best we can do is make generalized, careful discernments about particular acts of communication.

Discerning the appropriateness of mediums is an imprecise effort. But rather than rise to the challenge, evangelicals have often chosen to focus on the lowest, although essential, criterion: is it expressing a biblical truth? By that criterion, the most ridiculous Christian parody T-shirt can pass as long as a biblical verse is somehow woven into the parody. We can do better.

There are some sensible questions we can ask ourselves as we seek to communicate our faith. These questions are far from exhaustive and are best used in community so multiple people can offer their interpretation, with the understanding that no one interpretation is authoritative:

1. What kinds of messages is this medium typically used to convey?

2. What connotations, images, and connections will people make with this message in this medium?

3. Am I communicating the truth of my message in this form?

4. Will others perceive the radical uniqueness of this message, or will they categorize it as yet another consumer choice?

The way we speak, write, and visually depict our faith has a serious effect on the way others conceive of the nature of faith. Words like *sin, redemption, guilt,* and *grace* are tied up with the rhetorical shape we give them. And if that shape takes its source from a secular marketplace, we can expect the words to be heard as part of that marketplace. By asking these basic questions about how mediums convey messages, we can begin to distinguish our faith.

AN EXAMPLE OF FAILING TO CARRY THE MESSAGE: VBS

I don't think most of us have a sense of how much we trivialize our faith in our evangelical churches. This fact was brought home to me recently when I observed a Vacation Bible School program from one of the most popular suppliers of prepackaged VBS programs. The theme of the program was understanding God as Creator—delighting in his creation, knowing that we were made for a reason, and giving thanks. Like most such curricula, this one came with a script, decorations, a set, songs, videos, and lesson plans. Considering the incredible amount of work needed to teach, entertain, and wrangle small children for several hours a day, these prepackaged programs are very valuable. They allow churches with few resources to put on a program with high production values—which is important when you're competing for the attention of children (and parents!) who are used to having easy access to glossy, high-speed entertainment. It's not hard to see why churches would be hesitant to critique the way a VBS program *carries the message* of the gospel, so long as it does carry it. After all, these programs dramatically lower the time and cost of VBS, and they can provide any church with a professional, high-tech program. But it's possible for sincere, theologically grounded men and women to selflessly give their time to teach children about God, all while unintentionally reinforcing visions of God that are simply untrue.

In the sanctuary, the stage was decorated with gears and wheels of various sizes and colors, and over them a sign announced the name of the VBS program. On the floor were cans, cables, and odds and ends that represented an inventor's workshop. Cardstock gears were hung through the halls. The theme of this program was that God is our Creator, and he made us for a reason—but the dominant image used to convey this idea was a gear. Rather than the beautiful, awesome, mysterious God of Genesis, the imagery recalled the Divine Watchmaker of early nineteenth-century deism.

At the start of the program, the leader, reading from a script, asked the kids to share their "God sightings"—observations of something beautiful or good in God's creation. Helping children get into the habit of seeing creation *as* creation is a noble and praiseworthy purpose for any VBS. After the first child shared her God sighting, all the other kids said in unison, as rehearsed, "Wow, God." Their lack of enthusiasm was so complete that the first time I heard it, I thought they were being sarcastic: "Oh, 'Wow, God,' you put a squirrel in Susan's yard. Way to go." That's the thing about interjections: it's very difficult to say them sincerely unless you really are struck by something. We can't recite awe on cue: it bursts out of us when we're confronted by something worthy of awe. It strikes us *viscerally*, not intellectually, and it breaks through the detached rationalism of the buffered self. The proper response to awe is gratitude (remember the double movement). But sitting inside that sanctuary, surrounded by cartoonish cardstock gears, the kids' "wows" sounded phony. There was nothing there to *move* them.

Next they watched a short video narrated by a CGI owl who talked about how real owls survive in the wild. The video included some nice footage of owls and some interesting facts. It was a bit like a five-minute Animal Planet show with a loosely related verse at the end. Although it was good to see an example of God's creation, there was still nothing really wonderful about it. Between the cartoon owl narrator, the factoid-filled script, and the quick cuts that prevented us from really looking at the owls, there was no sense of majesty or mystery. On the contrary, nature was contained, cartooned, and scientifically described. Oh, and the kids could take the cartoon owl home with them on a little tag that could be read by an iPad or iPhone with the proper app, so that after VBS was over, they could learn more about God's creation indoors, staring at a screen.

If my description of this VBS program feels a bit harsh, that's because we need to see just how absurd this all is. Here we are trying to teach our children that they are fearfully and wonderfully made by a great Creator God who made and sustains all things by his powerful Word—so we spend hundreds of dollars to *mediate* that creation and suck every bit of wonder and mystery and beauty out of it we possibly can. And why? Because culturally, that's just what we do.

Our society doesn't recognize the wonder and beauty of creation. We see "Curious Creatures," "Marvelous Mammals," "Deadly Dinos!" and other silly alliterations, but we don't often bother looking at the thing itself. We have plenty of factoids about insects, plenty of shocking videos of predators, and plenty of quick-cut TV shows with overly excited animal experts and thrill seekers emoting about nature, but we are not so keen on being here and seeing it ourselves. We've got to be climbing it or biking it or running it or conquering it or jumping off it—in other words we can *use* it, but it's hard for us to *delight* in it. Perhaps this is because if we believed that even the little tree in our front yard is a miracle, we'd have to spend all day in gratitude to God. We'd have to pray without ceasing.

This program presented creation to children in a familiar, attractive medium. The message spoke of God's beautiful creation, but the medium hid that beauty. I have no doubt that the children who attended this VBS heard the gospel and were loved and cared for by godly, selfless brothers and sisters in

Christ—and for that, I rejoice. But that doesn't change the fact that the program worked hard and used the latest technology and media to avoid doing the one thing it set out to do: reveal the wonder of creation.

EXCARNATION

After we have recognized and begun to move away from cultural practices that conflate Christianity with lifestyle choices or otherwise trivialize the faith, we can begin to replace them with practices, mediums, and aesthetics that more honestly convey the embodied solemnity and awe that is appropriate before God. To help us see more clearly the ways in which non-Christian ideas have crept into our church services, we can turn to Charles Taylor's concept of "excarnation."

As Western culture has shifted its focus inward, toward disengaged reason, Taylor sees a parallel move within Christianity—a move from embodied forms of religious worship to those in which religion is essentially something that only happens in your head.[1] Taylor calls this move "excarnation," since it devalues and nearly erases the role of our bodies in worship. Consider his description of modern culture, including modern Christianity.

Modern enlightened culture is very theory-oriented. We tend to live in our heads, trusting our disengaged understandings: of experience, of beauty (we can't really accept that it's telling us anything, unless about our own feelings); even the ethical: we think that the only valid form of ethical self-direction is through rational maxims or understanding.

We can't accept that part of being good is opening ourselves to certain feelings; either the horror at infanticide, or agape as a gut feeling.[2]

Taylor notes that not all expressions of Christianity have adopted excarnation, but in general, it is true that our church services (especially in evangelicalism) involve less liturgy, less focus on bodily participation, and greater emphasis on disengaged reason. Reading Taylor's description, I can't help but think of experiences I've had in evangelical churches: the overwhelming sense that the *real* point of church is to receive a good lecture about the Bible that I can rationally apply to an area of my life to improve my standing before God, or my happiness, or my understanding of this lifestyle I identify with.

But broadly speaking, I suspect that Taylor is right about most expressions of contemporary Christian faith: we have made communion with God a thing that happens inside our heads, not with our whole selves, including our bodies. To find evidence of this we only have to look at "online churches," "satellite campuses," the normalization of smartphone use during services, and the lack of participation expected of congregations. And if the purpose of church is to learn about God the way we learn about any other subject, we shouldn't be surprised when people stop showing up to church once they feel they've learned everything. I've heard this sentiment expressed many times, and have felt the same way myself. After a while, particularly if you remain in one church for several years, you feel like you've heard everything the pastor has to say. After that, going to church feels like attending the same Christianity 101 course semester after semester. Why bother? Well, we're told, because we need to be reminded of these basic facts. And that's true. One of the major themes of the Old Testament is that humans are forgetful, almost hopelessly so. But if I've heard all the main variations of sermons and I just need a reminder, it's not necessary to drive all the way to church. Downloading the sermon later in the day and listening while I do the dishes should be sufficient. Besides, my tithe is automatically donated each month from my checking account, and we only celebrate Communion the first Sunday of the month. (I don't want to put too fine a point on this, but for a parent of three small children, going to church is a huge challenge.) The weekly gathering together of saints is only justified if attending church is about much more than intellectual growth. In this sense, excarnation is not only a deviation from historical Christianity. It also renders regular church attendance obsolete.

Taylor has some suggestions for how to address excarnation in the church: "The aim is . . . to find new forms of collective rituals; rites of passage; individual and small group disciplines of prayer, fasting, devotion; modes of marking time; new ways of living conjugal sexual life; new ways of healing and sharing, which could give bodily and at times public expression to the worship of God."[3] The church has the historical resources to do just this. We have collective rituals of Communion, baptism, church membership, and marriage; disciplines of prayer, fasting, and devotion; and holy days, all of which "give bodily and at times public expression to the worship of God." We must set about restoring, reframing, and revitalizing these practices in light of the incarnation.

For this, we can turn to James K. A. Smith and his Cultural Liturgies series, in which he addresses this very question. In what follows, we will look at some of Smith's recommendations for embodied worship, with some additions of my own, and draw attention to the ways these practices can challenge our distracted, secular age.

In the first volume of his Cultural Liturgies series, *Desiring the Kingdom*, Smith argues that modern Christians have put far too much emphasis on encouraging believers to believe the right things, rather than shaping what we love and therefore desire through liturgies, which Smith defines as "rituals of ultimate concern."[4] We are "liturgical animals," Smith writes, and we learn far more about the world through our habitual experiences than we modern people like to admit. In *Desiring the Kingdom* and the second volume, *Imagining the Kingdom*, Smith shows how we learn through our bodies, how stories shape our loves, and—most important for the purposes of this book— how church services can be ordered to form our loves toward God more fully. While Smith is not specifically focused on the ways in which embodied worship can function as a disruptive witness to a distracted, secular age, his rich exegesis of Christian worship does just that. Smith devotes an entire chapter to the major steps in the traditional liturgy of the church, explaining what it involves, how it rightly incorporates our bodies, and how the entirety of the liturgy functions as a narrative that retells the gospel story.

THE CHURCH SERVICE

Beginning with the environment of worship, specifically the use of liturgical colors to mark the movement of the liturgical calendar through seasons like Advent and Lent, Smith says, "just the space of worship would tell a story that actually organizes time—an indication that here dwells a people with a unique sense of the *temporality*, of commercial time or the standard shape of the academic year."[5] One of the defining features of the secular world is that people cease to recognize what Charles Taylor calls "high times"—sacred times of communal celebration. The feasts in the Old Testament are an ancient example, as is the calendar of the church as it was practiced in the Middle Ages, and still is today in many Christian traditions. The key to these "high times" is that their meaning and order was imposed externally by a transcendent source. This provided a cosmic rhythm to life.

Today we conceive of time in almost purely indifferent, mechanical terms. It is a naked measurement, so that whatever meaning we have in the rhythms of our lives is entirely self-imposed or (at best) imposed by society. And if it's the latter, it almost always takes the form of commercial meaning (Father's Day, Valentine's Day) or political meaning (Tax Day, Fourth of July). But the practice of attending church weekly and moving through the cycle of Christ's birth, life, crucifixion, death, and resurrection reorients us and reminds us that there is a way of being in the world that is truer than the sense of life we have within the immanent frame.

While most church practices take place within the walls of the church building, and thus outside the public's view, the Advent season is unusually public. In fact, it's one of the few religious times of year recognized and celebrated (in some sense) with enthusiasm by non-Christians. As the processes of secularization, individualism, and globalism have crept on, most communities in the West have had fewer and fewer shared holidays, let alone seasons. Again, time has been robbed of its natural cadences and instead appears as the raw material we use to cultivate our own identities. And yet, right after Thanksgiving, the nation undergoes a massive transformation. Decorations go up, and our musical playlists, clothes, and greetings all change. Families return home to be with one another. Companies give their employees bonuses and time off. Stores close. Cities decorate their streets with lights. The normal flow of life is altered.

Nothing captures this change so powerfully as Christmas lights. For about a month the night sky is lit up with color, enchanting the suburbs and hinting at a transcendent truth: *this time is not like other times*. What makes the Advent season stand out so starkly is that our culture has virtually no other holy days left. No other holiday reshapes our collective imagination for so long. Christmas disrupts nearly every part of our society, so we are left believing it must signify *something*. The Advent season is capable of forcing people to see there is more to being than the pull of modern secular consumerist life. However, as Charlie Brown reminds us every year, Christmas is constantly co-opted for secular purposes that work to undermine whatever disruptive force the season still retains.

While I don't believe it's possible for secularization to completely stifle the otherness of the holiday, it does pose a challenge for the church if we are to have a disruptive witness. Here we have a season that disrupts our lives and points to a reality beyond our preferences and distracted lives, so the question becomes, What Advent practices can we adopt that will help us and others sense the reality of the transcendent? How can we take these commercialized intimations of an otherworldly order to time and reframe them within the true narrative of Christ's incarnation? I believe the answer involves practices and events that carry the solemnity, joy, and beauty of Christ's birth. Not gimmicks, excessive pageantry, or grand concerts that draw people's attention to our high production values, but events that encourage the double movement—moving people out of their heads to meditate on the story of the incarnation, and ultimately upward to God with thanksgiving.

Continuing the theme of being drawn out of ourselves, Smith looks at the Greeting of Peace, the time when churches pause and asks congregants to greet one another. The reason "we extend mutual greetings [is] because God has welcomed us."[6] This is another example of the double movement: we receive God's welcome, but the telos of his love for us never remains in us; it should always go forth to our neighbors, who also bear God's image, and in that sense, back to God. Notice too that this is an embodied activity. In some churches it is more embodied than others. We stand up, move around, shake hands, hug one another, look each other in the eye, and say, "The peace of Christ be with you." As someone who feels himself to be growing more introverted with age, who is often stressed and exhausted from wrestling with his children to get them ready for church, and who occasionally suffers from a mental illness, I confess that I dislike the Greeting of Peace. I don't want to greet you. The entire thing makes me uncomfortable and irritated. If you'd like to chat with me after church, I'd be happy to do that, but to get out of my seat and move around and speak God's peace and shake hands, it's all too much for me. I want to stay in my head. But this is precisely the point. Worshiping God is not something I accommodate to myself.

I would venture to say that if you are attending a healthy church that uses traditional liturgical elements and you spend any meaningful amount of time in the wider culture, you will discover some aspect of the service that makes you similarly uncomfortable. Part of that discomfort is the experience of having your vision of the world reformed. I will likely always be introverted, but I should not always feel that the privacy of my head is the safest and best place to be. In welcoming one another, Smith writes, "We are immediately reminded that worship is not a private affair; we have gathered as a people, as a congregation, and just as together we are dependent on our redeeming Creator, so too are we dependent on one another." Smith notes that "such dependence is part of the very fiber of God's good creation."[7] Face to face, we are compelled to exercise and vocalize the reality that we live dependent on God's sustaining power, and that we are also dependent on one another. We are drawn outside of our heads and outside of our visions of self-sufficiency and autonomy.

According to Smith, singing in worship is likewise properly understood as an embodied act.[8] When we sing we must stand and use our body to publicly express praise to God. And although singing involves a cognitive component—the lyrics carry theological meaning—that meaning is inseparable from the form of the song and its expression through my vocal chords. And singing at church is not a private affair: "The practice of singing together in Christian worship—singing *one* song, with different parts, in harmony—is a small but significant performance of what we're looking forward to in the kingdom."[9] In this way, singing is another reminder of the spiritual reality of the body of Christ, his church. Our tendency is to conceptualize the body of Christ, treating it purely as a kind of metaphor for the diversity of the church, something like the way businesses tell their employees that they are part of a family or team. The difference is that the church *really is* the body of Christ on earth. It is both figurative and literal. We are joined together through Christ across time and space in a way that simply is not true of any business team. Through singing together, we enact this mystery in worship of God.

My own experience of singing in church has rarely reflected these realities. I usually experience worship as an individual who just happens to be singing around other individuals. This sense is only heightened by the general lack of full-throated singing in many churches. Without delving too deeply into the worship wars, part of the challenge of contemporary services is that our focus is directed to the stage rather than to one another. Volume levels rarely allow us to hear ourselves clearly, and certainly not our neighbors. The result is that we experience worship much like we experience a concert. It becomes an individual, emotional, and spiritual exercise wherein I try my best to think about the words and praise God. But even though I am surrounded by the saints, I remain comfortably in my own head.

The most moving worship experience I have had is when a church I attended in California sang a Christmas hymn together. We sang together as a congregation every Sunday morning, but the reality was that the worship team usually drowned us. Because of this, and the fact that style and tone of the songs often fit so poorly with their lyrics, I would regularly arrive late for church just to skip the music. But that Christmas the congregation sang with such fervor and conviction that I felt spiritually united with a people across time and space, and through those people to a historical and transcendent truth: Jesus Christ became human and died on the cross for the forgiveness of my sins. I think this was the first time I experienced "addressing one another in psalms and hymns and spiritual songs" (Ephesians 5:19). To "address one another" we must be able to hear one another. This is not curmudgeonly complaining about the music being too loud; rather, it is a point about the relational *function* of worship. We certainly need to look for theologically and aesthetically rich songs, and to work toward musical excellence as we lead the worship. But if our worship remains an individual spiritual exercise, we will have failed to follow Paul's command in Ephesians and will contribute instead to the secular trend of reducing the spiritual to the private.

Although it is not practiced often in most evangelical churches, as Smith describes it, the announcement of the law, whether it be from the Ten Commandments or the Gospels, reorients our moral vision toward God. As we have discussed in the first part of this book, one of the qualities of our times is that our world-views tend to be fragmented, frail, and incoherent. We adopt ethical stances in response to social pressures and compelling media narratives, with little regard for how these ethics fit with our overall vision of the world. There is a *lightness* to our morality, even though we may be quite passionate about expressing it. This is morality within the immanent frame, morality mapped by corporate interests, trending topics, convenience, and expressive individualism. The weekly practice of reading a portion of God's law helps reorient us, not just to the particulars of Christian ethics but to the radical idea that these laws transcend us and our society, and yet are built into the fabric of creation.

> The announcement of the law and the articulation of God's will for our lives signals that our good is not something that we determine or choose for ourselves. The secular liturgies of late modern culture are bent on forming in us a notion of autonomy—a sense that we are a law unto ourselves and that we are only properly "free" when we can choose our own ends, determine our own *telos*.[10]

The "secular liturgy" (Smith's term) of shopping in a consumer society instills in us a sense that we *do* "choose our own ends" through purchases. Consumerism trains us to think of ourselves as choosing beings. Everything is an option, and we define ourselves by our choices. Once habituated to choice, we squirm under the prospect of moral authority. Taylor notes, "For many people today, to set aside their own path in order to conform to some external authority just doesn't seem comprehensible as a form of spiritual life."[11] The reading of the law offers a liturgical corrective, one needed for those within the church as much as those without. It challenges our habit of personal choice with a habit of communal affirmation that an external authority forms our morality, not our personal preferences.

Public and silent confession, along with the assurance of pardon, particularly when practiced weekly, requires the self-reflection and honesty so essential to the good life. Whatever our personal devotion time looks like, a time of silent confession in church helps cultivate a habit of honest self-reflection. During the confession of sins, we read together a general confession and then silently seek the Holy Spirit's discernment and reflect on our personal sins, identifying those we might have been denying all week. This is a powerful moment of equality. Everyone, young and old, rich and poor, pastor and child, is in need of God's grace. Everyone is in need of forgiveness. Everyone is a sinner. The meritocracy of American society is dashed upon the realities of the fall and of God's love for us. And, as Smith explains, confession gives us a different way to understand guilt from the prevailing social narratives: "In confession and assurance of pardon, we meet a moment where Christian worship runs counter to the formation of secular liturgies that either tend to nullify talk of guilt and responsibility or tend to point out failures without extending assurance of pardon."[12] As with the announcement of the law, confession and the assurance of pardon are *actions* (we speak, bow, stand, and speak) that form our moral vision in line with God's. And the physical and communal aspects of these movements work against the tendency toward excarnation. Confession and repentance take place in our minds, but they are also vocalized.

Of all the movements in a church liturgy, the two that perhaps most strongly challenge life in a closed, immanent frame are prayer and the Lord's Supper, because at their core is communion with a living God. Smith articulates the power of prayer in a secular age.

> Perhaps this is the first thing we should note about the practice of prayer with respect to the Christian social imaginary: it is a practice that makes us people who refuse to settle for appearances. Or, to put it otherwise, it makes us a people who always see that there's more going on than meets the eye. One might even say it's another indication that for Christians who pray, the world must be characterized by a kind of enchantment.[13]

In prayer we affirm our contingency: we are sustained in this world only by Christ's hand. We affirm our dependency on others. We affirm our obligations to consider the needs of others. We affirm the reality of being beyond the material world. We affirm that the order of natural laws, bureaucracy, and technology do not contain or define being in the world. There is a being who loves us, who longs to commune with us, and who supersedes all earthly principalities. And we affirm all of this together, as a body.

Smith claims that the way to our heart is through stories that affect us "at a gut level" and that "seep into our background in order to then shape our perception of the world.[14] If this is true, then sermons that are grounded in the Scriptures should always be part of the story of God's revelation of love. Here, as throughout the service, intentional solemnity is important to convey the sacredness of the Word. By solemnity I do not mean sternness. The church is good at being stern about sin, but it's often less good at being solemn before God's holiness. In part, this is because self-discipline is perfectly compatible with the spirit of detached rationalism of our age. We learn the law, judge ourselves and others, and take rational steps to improve our behavior. But solemnity is different. It does not require us to be grim or harsh, and its focus is not on self-improvement. It asks merely that we recognize the sacredness of the act of opening God's Word—the fact that it is a means of grace for our sanctification.

We can be solemn and still find room in a sermon for humor and certainly for joy, but all this must be done without trivializing the Word or the office of elder. The mood of a Christian worship service, including the sermon, should capture the truth of the living God and the exclusivity of his path. As a young Christian, I was anxious to "feel God's presence," fearing that if I couldn't feel it, then perhaps I was not truly right with God. To bear a disruptive witness in a distracted, secular age, we do not need to *feel* the presence of God, but we ought to sense that this is a place where Christ has come to meet his people. The service conveys the awesomeness of God's presence in his Word and the sacraments, whether or not we have an inward experience of God's presence.[15]

It's hard to imagine an act more disruptive to secularism than celebrating the Lord's Supper. Every movement in the liturgy of the Lord's Supper calls us away from a distracted, flattened, material, individualist, and secular view of the world. The reading from the Gospel grounds the sacrament not in mythology or doctrine but in time and space, and it rips us out of our presentism. We are joined with saints across two thousand years, hearing these same words and partaking in the same sacrament because of one God-man and his words and deeds: "On the night when he was betrayed [the Lord Jesus] took bread, and when he had given thanks, he broke it, and said, 'This is my body, which is for you. Do this in remembrance of me'" (1 Corinthians 11:23-24). By grounding the Lord's Supper thoroughly in ancient history, our faith unsettles our complacency in the present. It reminds us that *now* is not all there ever was. In many traditions, including my own Presbyterian strain, the liturgy entails proclaiming "the mystery of our faith," and the entire congregation as one body says, "Christ has died, Christ has risen, Christ will come again." The sweep through time (the past where Christ died and rose again, the present in which we proclaim, and the future which we anticipate) is both a statement of what Christians believe and a proclamation, the kind of speech that does not merely observe a fact but calls it our own.

This understanding of our faith defies a secular perspective because its grounding is thoroughly external, even as it resonates inside us. The mystery of faith is in Christ's actions in history, in the present, and in the future. And the public proclamation of this, combined with the bread and the wine, enacts this faith. In the partaking of the bread and the wine, we participate in objective, bodily events. They are not individual or private, although they do affect us personally. In the Lord's Supper we partake of the body and blood of Christ in a spiritually objective event in which God communes with us and feeds us. The Lord's Supper involves remembering what Christ did, but it is not merely recollection, for that would be private and cognitive. If recollecting Christ's sacrifice cognitively were the only purpose of the sacrament, then we would do just as well skipping those tiny plastic cups and wafers that taste like cardboard and simply recite the Scriptures instead. But thanks be to God, that is not the only purpose. In partaking of the Lord's Supper, we mysteriously, spiritually, but all the same *truly* partake in Christ, and this event has a real effect on us and our spirits. The Lord's Supper is profoundly at odds with a secular understanding of the world, which has no space or even any language for an event so miraculous and meaningful and irreducible. By keeping Christ's command to take the Lord's Supper, we are presenting a sign to ourselves and to our watching neighbors that there are truer, fuller ways of being in the world.

The image of worship that Smith articulates in *Desiring the Kingdom* is a powerfully disruptive witness, working against our habits of distraction by involving our bodies and minds intentionally in worship, and working against the influence of secularism by asserting a faith that transcends time, people, place, and creation while simultaneously asserting the goodness of creation through the incarnation.

Aside from reforming our liturgy, we need to consider the creeping influence of a distracted age upon church services as a whole. In churches, as well as schools, leaders struggle to engage people who have been formed by continual distraction. Can a congregation with no attention span partake in a five-minute prayer? Shamefully, I admit to cringing at the idea of five minutes of silence, of eyes closed, of listening to my pastor and making his petition my petition to God. I used the word *shameful* here because I know how fleeting five minutes are when I am on my phone or on social media. How is it that we have allowed ourselves to be so acculturated to distraction and stimulation that we grow agitated at a pastor who prayed for five minutes?

Sermons are no better, but with them the problem is less that we cannot stand their length as we cannot resist being distracted during them. The convenience of Bible apps has caused many church goers to stop bringing their Bibles to church, but the great temptation is that there is always something else you can do on your phone once it is opened. Sometimes we can justify our distraction from the sermon: *I wonder what that word means in the original Greek. I'd better tweet that quote before I forget it. My followers would be blessed by it!* But in all cases the norming of technology use in church services has made it easier for us to not be present. In addition, it makes preaching God's Word (a means of grace!) into just another thing we can choose to engage at that moment. My point with this aside is to suggest that churches make intentional decisions about how to encourage healthy cognitive habits in their congregations by setting etiquette standards, by giving space for self-reflection, and by pushing for longer periods of prayer. Practically this might look like asking people to shut off and put away all cellphones for the duration of the service. It may also mean avoiding the use of video and graphics that stimulate rather than invite people to meditate. The distractions of life and children are more than enough to make being present a challenge for most

Christians. Churches should do what they can to create a culture that minimizes the other distractions.

CONCLUSION

The church's practices offer the world something that is unsettling and yet speaks to our longing for meaning, order, and transcendence. But these practices should not be pursued with the goal of appearing spiritual. There is no value in being a Jesus Freak merely to be a freak. We are called to a much higher standard. The traditional liturgical elements of a church service have a goodness and beauty in them that we ought to pursue regardless of their effectiveness as evangelism. Considering a disruptive witness can help us shape these practices so they emphasize what is true about our faith. As we have seen, the church already has the resources to disrupt the habits and thought patterns cultivated in a distracted, secular age. The question is whether we will use what God has given us.

However, if we choose to use the liturgical forms available to us through Christian tradition to intentionally disrupt the distractions of modern life and the immanent frame, we will do much more than create a counterformation to secular culture (although that in itself is a worthy goal). Practiced along with the personal habits described in chapter four, our church liturgies will change the way we conceive of God, his presence in the world, and the gospel. Our doctrinal commitments may not change, but the background assumptions that shape our experience and imagination should more truly conform to the reality of God's love, creation, incarnation, resurrection, and redemption of humanity. These truths should be more viscerally real.

Many of the barriers to bearing witness to our faith described in the first part of this book begin to break down as we allow the practices discussed in chapters four and five to permeate our lives. When our church liturgy captures the solemnity and transcendence of God, it will naturally begin to reform the way we speak of him outside of church. When the aesthetics of the church shun secular marketing and media trends that trivialize the faith, we naturally will be more inclined to convey the uniqueness of the gospel. And when the double movement becomes our habit of being, bearing witness can cease to be a rhetorical game we play to affirm our identity and instead be focused outward on loving our neighbors through the gospel.

In other words, our personal and church practices bear witness to the watching world that we worship a loving God, but they also prepare us to enter into dialogue with our unbelieving neighbors in ways that better carry the gospel of Jesus Christ.

6

DISRUPTIVE CULTURAL PARTICIPATION

The student who followed me to my office after class was clearly shaken. For a host of reasons, it is not uncommon for students to experience a mental health crisis while in college, and I thought he might be suffering from one. I prepared to encourage him, to remind him that his worth was hidden in Christ and not determined by grades, and to recommend our school's counseling services.

But when we sat down in my office, he told me that the novels we had been reading in class were really weighing on him. Teaching twentieth-century literature, I was used to hearing things like this. The world is a bleak place, particularly in twentieth-century literature. War, meaninglessness, emptiness, existential dread, absurdity, violence, chaos, nihilistic humor, moral decay—it's a difficult literary period to dwell in for any meaningful length of time; then again, our world is a difficult place to dwell in for any meaningful length of time.

He went on to say that these books were weighing on him because they resonated with him so deeply. "I'm an atheist," he told me, "and the thoughts and reasoning of the characters in these novels are the exact thoughts I've had, years ago. But I pushed them away. I just stopped thinking about them for years, until this class. Now I can't get away from it. And it scares me." In the modernist texts we were reading, he encountered characters who felt the emptiness of a disenchanted world and absurdly fought to impose meaning on it anyway. The electronic buzz of the twenty-first century allowed him to be buffered from his own fears of meaninglessness, until Conrad's *Heart of Darkness*, Camus's "The Guest," and Hemingway's *The Sun Also Rises* punctured that buffer and revealed the cross pressure between what he believed to be a meaningless world and his longing for meaning and hope. I asked him to consider the possibility that existence was meaningful and ordered by a loving God, and so we talked about that God. The rest of this story is not mine to tell.

CROSS PRESSURES

There are moments in our lives when we feel the tension between modern life as we know it within the immanent frame and our awareness of or longing for some vision of fullness that goes beyond it. It's the tension between feeling that "all things are continuing as they were since the beginning" and a hope in the "promise of his coming" (2 Peter 3:4). In these moments we are invited to consider the possibility that we are not at the center of the universe, that creating and expressing our identity is not our greatest purpose, that goodness may not be a preference but may be embodied in God, and that meaning is not primarily a choice of interpretation but a revelation.

We are invited to consider these things, but we almost always decline, or we recast this anxiety into the larger story of our journey toward self-actualization. Two places where we feel this tension most acutely are in the stories we tell, which play imaginatively on our suppressed desire for eternity, and in experiences of tragedy, which force us to face death and meaninglessness. By carefully identifying these moments of what Charles Taylor calls cross pressures, we can invite others to enter into reflection rather than distraction, and thus bear witness to the beauty, grace, and contingency of life in a way that disrupts the assumptions of secularism and gives glory to God.

Although it has become harder to believe in God in an age when the closed, immanent frame feels so natural to us, this doesn't mean that we are comfortable or content. Many of us suffer from the "malaise of immanence," a sense of meaninglessness in response to a flat and absurd world.[1] And we also must deal with cross pressures: "The whole culture experiences cross pressures, between the draw of the narratives of closed immanence on one side, and the sense of their inadequacy on the other, strengthened by encounter with existing milieu of religious practice, or just by some intimations of the transcendent."[2] We cope with this pressure in various ways. Christians may turn to books on apologetics to buttress their faith, or they may become more immersed in their local church, or remember God's faithfulness in their lives.[3] Likewise, when non-Christians encounter "some intimations of the transcendent," whether it be a powerful experience of the goodness of creation or a longing for perfect justice or a film that resonates with our desire for existential justification, they have many ways to interpret their encounter from within the immanent frame.

The result is what Taylor calls an immanent transcendence: an experience or thing that gives one the sense of going beyond the closed, immanent frame—but only the sense.[4] They may channel their experience with creation into an ethical obligation to care for nature or reframe it as a sublime awareness of humanity's ability to overcome, define, and control nature. A longing for perfect justice can easily be transformed into an entirely this-worldly effort to achieve justice. And the desire for existential validation evoked by a film can be placed on immanent goals: marriage, career advancement, wealth, fame, health, and the like. In each case, we have to *do* something with this desire for transcendence. And in the space where people decide how to interpret "intimations of the transcendent," Christians may offer interpretations commensurate with our experience, rather than immanent transcendence, which necessarily requires an impoverished vision of transcendence.

Taylor identifies three points of contact where these cross pressures are most keenly felt: our human agency, our moral obligations, and our aesthetic experiences.[5] What creates the pressure is the sense that these three realities of human experience are inadequately explained within a strictly closed immanence: "A major question for all positions which take their stand in immanence, whether materialistic or not, is: how can one account for the specific force of creative agency, or ethical demands, or for the power of artistic experience, without speaking in terms of some transcendent being or force which interpellates us?"[6]

Taylor appeals not to a logical inconsistency per se, but what we might call an existential, embodied, or felt inconsistency: "Art, Nature moves us; we have a deeper sense of meaning; we can't see our 'aesthetic' responses as just another form of pleasurable reaction. They have a deeper significance."[7] If the idea of a "felt inconsistency" seems silly or irrational, recall that Taylor (like James K. A. Smith, Emmanuel Mounier, Matthew B. Crawford, and many other philosophers of our time) is working under the assumption that we are not brains in vats. We don't just know things with our minds alone but with and through our bodies. And so we might have an aesthetic (bodily!) experience with a novel or film or song that gives us a kind of *knowledge* about existence that is inconsistent with our basic assumptions about existence. We might, for example, be moved by a slave narrative like *Narrative of the Life of Frederick Douglass* to see the evil of slavery in a way that a logical argument about the injustice of slavery simply could not convey. Or *The Great Gatsby* may awaken our latent desire for eternal and perfect validation by another person, even though we believe in utter self-sufficiency.

The test for our beliefs is whether they can account for existence as we know it. And in the case of art and nature, it's whether they can account for our experience of these things without impoverishment. Taylor writes, "There are certain works of art—by Dante, Bach, the makers of Chartres Cathedral: the list is endless—whose power seems inseparable from their epiphanic, transcendent reference. Here the challenge is to the unbeliever, to find a non-theistic register in which to respond to them without impoverishment."[8] Taylor's argument is compelling because it requires us to find an account of existence that best fits with the things in life that matter to us most: love, beauty, morality, agency. In a way, Taylor takes the scientific question "What hypothesis best fits the evidence?" and applies it to subjects outside of the purview of science. The elements of life that most make it worth living, that grant it meaning and significance, demand an account that does them justice. And as Taylor observes, a closed, immanent account of reality can offer only an immanent transcendence at best.

Besides aesthetics, the other two points of pressure listed by Taylor are personal agency and morality—and in tragedy both of these meet. The goodness of our personhood is curtailed by suffering or death; the creative romantic relationship we have cultivated is randomly and unjustly ended in death; and our suffering reveals to us our mortality and the burden of discovering sufficient meaning in life to validate our existence: "All joy strives for eternity, because it loses some of its sense if it doesn't last."[9] Like art, tragedy—particularly the tragedy of a loved one's death—has a way of putting our commitments to the immanent frame under pressure. In tragedy we face an end to joy that defies our sense of what joy *is*: "Suffering can make plain to us some of the meaning of life which we couldn't appreciate before."[10] All our efforts to suppress the reality of death, suffering, and loss will eventually be undone by life, forcing us at least momentarily into the stark light of day where we acutely feel the cross pressure of the immanent frame and the abiding sense that "joy strives for eternity." In Christianity, that striving finds its correspondence in a God who suffered and died so that we might live again.

When we embody this truth through our compassion, honesty, empathy, and abiding service to those experiencing tragedy, it is nothing less than a disruptive witness, defying our culture's denial of death.[11]

STORIES: TRANSCENDENCE, GRATITUDE, AND BEAUTY

Stories have a unique ability to tap into and evoke our desires for the transcendent. They reveal and accentuate cross pressures, and they appeal to us as whole persons through aesthetics. Well-made stories by Christians can open people to the possibility of a reality beyond the immanent frame—but even well-made stories by non-Christians that use allegories of transcendence can awaken us to our latent desire for the transcendent. When Christians interpret, critique, and discuss stories with our neighbors, we can model a contemplative approach that promotes self-reflection and honesty, inviting empathy rather than promoting the detached rationalism of the buffered self. We can lean into the cross pressures produced by these stories. We can offer interpretations that affirm and account for our longings for forms of beauty, goodness, order, and love that find their being beyond the immanent frame.

By "stories" I don't just mean novels. I'm referring to all the cultural works that involve narratives: films, TV shows, songs, albums, plays, commercials, video games, and so on. Obviously, most stories aren't thoughtful and compelling enough to invest time in, but there are a great many that are worthy of praise and attention. We *participate* in stories when we *receive* them charitably and *dialogue* with others about how to interpret them. Participation is the combined act of receiving (watching, listening, reading, seeing, etc.) and dialoguing (writing reviews, critiquing, arguing about a film's ending, etc.). According to this definition, virtually everyone in America is participating in stories every day—grandmothers who speculate about a cliffhanger on a soap opera, users who add annotations to lyrics on Genius.com, or friends discussing a film they just saw in a theater. Participating in stories is a vital part of culture, and it is not a coincidence that it has so much capacity to disrupt our understanding of the world.

These stories are attempts by fallen people to make some kind of sense of existence. At their best, stories are imaginative efforts to order our world and identify or create meaning in it, even if that meaning is that life is meaningless and our attempts to create meaning are absurd. Unlike other forms of communication, stories are embodied in that they portray worlds, not just ideas. They allow us to imagine how we might find meaning through self-expression or heroism. They allow us to question our vision of fullness and consider alternatives. And because stories can convey a world, they can help us imagine new paradigms, whole new ways of understanding life, like the possibility that there is reality beyond the immanent frame.

Given the ability of stories to create this space for imaginative reflection on meaning and existence, it shouldn't be surprising that Charles Taylor points to literature as one of the ways modern people can envision a paradigm shift out of the immanent frame.[12] Taylor argues that converting from something like a materialist view of the world to a spiritual one is not merely a change in beliefs. It involves changing our background assumptions about life. This kind of change requires new ways of speaking, new languages that resonate more fully with people who are deeply inured by the closed, immanent frame.

> Many of the great founding moves of a new spiritual direction in history involve a transformation of the frame in which people thought, felt and lived before. They bring into view something beyond that frame, which at the same time change the meaning of all the elements of the frame. Things make sense in a wholly new way.... There was something very disruptive of existing habits of thought, action, and piety.[13]

Asking people to see beyond the frame is extremely difficult, because the frame of the immanent world is our background assumption, and what we can't see is hard to look beyond. It takes a work of imagination to go beyond—a spiritual imagination. Stories provide the space for this imagining.

In a well-crafted story we not only rationally consider the vision of the world created by the artist or artists, we enter that world. And good storytelling invites us to empathize; we viscerally feel the world and the values and ideas that govern it. Stories provide models for ascribing meaning to our own lives, which makes stories ideal for the kind of disruption Taylor has in mind. His focus is specifically on how Christian authors and poets can help those of us stuck in the immanent frame to imagine a world beyond, without taking us *out* of this world in a gnostic fashion.[14]

But we can take Taylor's claim a step further. For those of us who are not artists, our *participation* in other people's stories can also "break from the immanent order to a larger, more encompassing one, which includes it while disrupting it."[15] Our interpretation and dialogue about stories can help our neighbors "feel the solicitations of the spiritual" as they appear in art.[16] Our cultural participation can challenge the buffered self by showing that "part of being good is opening ourselves to certain feelings; either the horror at infanticide, or agape as a gut feeling."[17] With discernment, charity, and dialogue, Christians can participate in stories in disruptive ways that challenge the distracted, secular age.

In concrete terms, this participation might involve going to a movie theater with a friend and talking about the film afterward, book clubs, discussing the latest episode of a TV show with a coworker, hosting parties for watching a TV show that intentionally include time for dialogue, hosting movie nights, or making time to talk about an album with a group of friends. Again, virtually all of us in America do this sort of thing to some extent. Stories of one kind or another are at the heart of our culture, and we relate to one another by sharing them and interpreting them together. I'm recommending that we be more intentional about our participation in stories in specific ways, in order to make the immanent frame more visible and to interpret intimations of transcendence toward the more satisfying and fulfilling account of existence found in Christ.

Practically, this means choosing aesthetically excellent stories, whether or not they are the most popular. These stories will tend to be darker or more depressing or heavy, which sounds unpleasant. But Christians should be known for their appreciation of tragedies, because in good tragedies we must reckon with our place in the world, the problem of evil, and the struggle for meaning. (In the classical sense of the term, *comedies* can also make us face these difficult realities, but in the contemporary world, this is less true.) All those questions and concerns our distracted age is good at helping us ignore come to the fore in stories that deal with the tragic element of life. I am not asking Christians to stop seeing superhero movies or listening to pop music, but we need to be mindful of how we use our time. Many of the popular stories in our culture leave us worse off. Instead of haunting us, they glorify vice, distract us from ourselves, lift our mood without lifting our spirits, and make us envious and covetous of fame, sexual conquests, and material possessions.

When a story haunts us, it troubles our buffered self; it intrudes on our thought life, makes connections to other stories and experiences and ideas, and compels us to contemplation. More often than not, this haunting is a manifestation of Taylor's cross pressures. This doesn't mean we should watch or read content we find objectionable or that we should only watch serious movies. A story that captures the beauty of creation or the imagination can haunt us just as much as a deadly serious story.

Every time I watch *Willy Wonka and the Chocolate Factory* I am haunted by Dahl's vision of wonder as captured so beautifully by Gene Wilder. Here is a world in which the immanent frame has a chocolate-factory-size hole in it. The final song in the movie, "Pure Imagination," is about retreating to a world of "pure imagination" where anything is possible, a world that Wonka calls "paradise." The lyrics (which were not written by Roald Dahl) are corny and heavy-handed, but with Wilder's sincerity, we begin to *feel* awaken within us a genuine longing for paradise, not unlike the experience of hearing Judy Garland sing "Over the Rainbow." When the song and the credits end, I am left with the feeling that there *ought* to be paradise, and I am reminded of C. S. Lewis's famous quote: "If I find in myself a desire which no experience in this world can satisfy, the most probable explanation is that I was made for another world."[18] We do not need to only participate in dark or troubling stories, but we do need to give priority to stories that haunt us, unsettle us, and expand us, whether through beauty and delight or tragedy.

We also need to make time and find space to interpret the stories through dialogue with others. Living in an atomistic culture, our default response to receiving a story is not to interpret it in community. We may have a personal opinion about it. We may tweet a 280-character review. We may debate parts of the story. But most of us are not inclined to take the time to slowly work through the meanings of the story in dialogue with one another. In other words, the prolonged, thoughtful, charitable dialogue about stories I'm recommending will not happen naturally. We need to intentionally pursue it.

The goal of this kind of dialogue is to reveal the points of cross pressure in the story, to consider the visions of fullness it portrays, and to relate it to the world as we know it. In the following section I'll use *The Great Gatsby* as an example of the kind of interpretation I have in mind, but first let me identify a few common evangelical approaches to cultural interpretation that we need to avoid.

I am not recommending that we participate in stories in order to find allegories for Christ or spiritual truths. This method doesn't take the world of the story seriously; it treats the story as a prop. Instead, we should consider what the story says about life and explore its truth in relation to our experience. This means we seriously and empathetically enter into the world of a story, even while we may deny the truths it conveys.

I am also not recommending that we participate in stories in order to show how non-Christians are wrong and sin is bad. Many years ago, I had a Christian student object to reading *The Great Gatsby* because, he said, "I don't need to read about people committing adultery and getting drunk to know that those things are sinful." Of course, he was right, in a way. If you read the novel *only* as a morality tale, you will be largely unsurprised. Likewise, if we watch movies by secular directors in order to point out how hopeless they are because they don't have Christ, we aren't treating them as people. They're props—evidence of how much better it is to be a Christian. And if we get to know enough Christians intimately, we will discover that many of them also suffer from bouts of hopelessness, mental illnesses, tragedy, and anxiety. We are followers of Christ because he loves us and called us to himself, not because we were promised a life of happiness. So playing the "whose life is better?" game is foolish and uncharitable. Good stories should produce empathy in us for others, regardless of who they are. Empathy does not mean that we affirm their actions or beliefs, but we understand and, as people who also suffer under sin, we lament. The correct posture for Christians approaching a story is one of humility, charity, and a desire to know. With such a posture, we treat our neighbors and the creators of the story as made in the image of

God, burdened by the same fallen world, and in need of the grace and mercy of the same Savior.

CASE STUDY: THE GREAT GATSBY

A thematic summary of F. Scott Fitzgerald's *The Great Gatsby* makes the novel sound tedious: First, the American dream of attaining wealth, fame, and romantic fulfillment through hard work is a deadly illusion. Second, idealizing a romantic interest will always let you down. Who doesn't already know this in 2018? Then again, who didn't know it in 1925? Students who have read the novel in high school have an especially difficult time re-reading it in college. Aside from some poetic language, the novel appears fairly obvious. Yet when we experience the novel (as opposed to this abstracted summary), when we allow ourselves to empathetically enter into Fitzgerald's world, it reveals things about our own hearts we are loath to acknowledge otherwise.

Part of Fitzgerald's genius is that he so evocatively captures the modern desire to place the "burden of godhead" (in Ernest Becker's terms) on someone we love. Phrased bluntly, it seems obvious that it's a terrible idea to allow our imagination to build up someone into a kind of deity. Of course we will be let down! But as Becker notes, this is precisely what we continue doing, over and over again. We imagine that if we could just be loved and accepted by this one, special, beautiful person, our lives would have fullness and meaning and existential validation. I don't think there's a single one of us who hasn't fantasized along these lines at some point in our life, whether the object of our desire is the girl who sat two seats away in English class or a singer in a boy band or a character in a film. We impose on them *transcendent* significance, by which I mean our image of them is irreducible to their material/biological/historical presence in the world. Here is Fitzgerald's depiction of Gatsby kissing Daisy, the woman he has "burdened with godhead."

> His heart beat faster and faster as Daisy's white face came up to his own. He knew that when he kissed this girl, and forever wed his unutterable visions to her perishable breath, his mind would never romp again like the mind of God. So he waited, listening for a moment longer to the tuning fork that had been struck upon a star. Then he kissed her. At his lips' touch she blossomed for him like a flower and the incarnation was complete.[19]

Note the cross pressure Gatsby suffers under. On the one side, he has his "unutterable vision" of Daisy, a vision of her as a kind of transcendent being who could grant him existential validation. On the other side is her "perishable breath," the stultifying knowledge that she is just as finite as everyone. She exists in an immanent frame, subject to the same laws of entropy and physics, destined to die just the same as anyone.

An empathetic and honest reader will recognize in themselves similar longings, if not for a romantic partner who can give their life validation, then for a career, a work of art, a sexual experience, an achievement, a status, a product—some vision of fullness that takes place within the immanent frame even while its significance extends far beyond it. Where does this desire come from? Why does it have such a force within our lives, driving a spouse to betray their marriage and family for the ideal of a lover's gaze, defining consumerism and marketing, motivating people to work themselves to death? Is there a being capable of bearing the weight of our desire for fullness? Could it be that Gatsby's longing for something irreducible to life in the immanent frame is not a story of the tragic absurdity of looking for meaning in a meaningless world, but rather it is a misdirected longing for the face of God?

These questions, elicited by a novel that resonates with most readers' experience with love and longing, invite us to contemplate our commitments, our perception of what is the highest good. By identifying and leaning into the cross pressures depicted in the text, we create a space to openly discuss this tension in our own lives, not from a position of superiority but from humility and charity—empathizing and lamenting with Gatsby, even if we do not share his answers.

For this case study, I chose a novel familiar to most Americans, but the practice of humbly participating in a story as an opportunity to contemplate and dialogue with neighbors about questions of meaning can just as well be applied to any number of mediums and stories. This dialogue serves as a disruptive witness by ploughing up the buffers we use to shield ourselves from self-reflection. In tragedy, we find ourselves similarly exposed.

TRAGEDY

"To be a human being one had to drink the cup," says Graham Greene's protagonist, Scobie, in *The Heart of the Matter*, capturing the inevitability of suffering in life.[20] For Scobie, who was forced to watch a six-year-old girl slowly die, it's not primarily our own suffering that makes this cup so bitter; it's the suffering of others, particularly those we love dearly. Charles Taylor argues that the loss of a loved one can make it "difficult to sustain a sense of the higher meaning of ordinary life,"[21] by which he means the belief that our ordinary lives have meaning and telos and value without reference to God or some other transcendent source. Why would the death of a loved one make it hard to sense that life has meaning? Taylor answers, "It's not just that they matter to us a lot, and hence there is a grievous hole in our lives when our partner dies. It's also because just because they are so significant, they seem to *demand eternity*."[22] This is especially true because relationships have become one of the sources of fullness in the modern world. With death, something that seemed *infinitely* meaningful is cut short, however hard we may try to memorialize them: "The deepest, most powerful kind of happiness, even in the moment, is plunged into a sense of meaning. And the meaning seems denied by certain kinds of ending."[23] Once again, Taylor is appealing to the *sense* of life, questioning what interpretations of existence impoverish those things we hold most dear, and what interpretations affirm what we know to be true and right. Death within the closed, immanent frame defies our embodied sense that personhood ought not have an end.[24] As a result, death feels incomprehensible.

Perhaps the most memorable scene in the 1994 film *Four Weddings and a Funeral* is the recitation of the poem "Funeral Blues" by W. H. Auden. In the film, the character Matthew recites the poem in honor of his partner, Gareth, who had died suddenly of a heart attack. Matthew tells the funeral attendees apologetically that he does not have the words to express his feelings, so he must rely on Auden to convey them for him. Aside from Auden's masterful use of language, the poem's power comes from its ability to describe what I've come to believe is a fundamental human experience of death, particularly in the last two lines: "Pour away the ocean and sweep up the wood; / For nothing now can ever come to any good."[25] In the previous lines, Auden calls for clocks to stop, for phone lines to be cut, for dogs to be silenced, for police officers to wear black gloves. Life, in other words, *ought* to stop because the man he loved is dead. The very idea that the world could go on with its business is surreal—death makes daily life surreal. Echoing Taylor's claim that love "demands eternity," Auden writes, "I thought love would last for ever; I was wrong." And precisely because it has *failed* to last forever, Auden feels that the world has a moral obligation to recognize the infinite loss of his love, for that would be a form of mourning commensurate with his loss.

One of my earliest experiences of death came when our family borrowed the 1985 PBS adaptation of Katherine Paterson's novel *Bridge to Terabithia*. It's the story of a boy and girl who become friends and play in a make-believe world together until the little girl, Leslie, drowns one day while visiting the world by herself. I must have only been thirteen or so, and I remember watching it one afternoon with no expectation that it was going to end tragically. When Leslie died it felt as if someone knocked all the air out of me. Even though it was early afternoon when the movie ended, I went to bed and lay there for a long time with a sick feeling in my stomach—an ache, an emptiness. My mom walked by my room vacuuming while I lay pondering the horrifying finality of death, and the juxtaposition of this banal housekeeping with my existential dread made me feel all the worse. How could my mother vacuum at a time like this? Didn't she know someone was dead? Couldn't she feel that absence? I wasn't mad at my mother, but I was recognizing a deep incongruity at the center of this life: each person's existence is infinitely significant because they are made in the image of a transcendent God, so when they die, their death ought to register throughout every square inch of the earth. As Auden wrote, the clocks should stop. So tremendous a thing is the death of a single person that we feel that the world ought to cease its motion. Being itself is contingent on the existence of each person—or at least, that's how it feels when someone dies.

In sociologist Peter Berger's short work *A Rumor of Angels*, he argues that there are prototypical human experiences that are "signals of transcendence," facts about our existence that make most sense, whose meaning are most fully articulated and justified through an appeal to the transcendent—namely, the existence of a good and loving God.[26] This sense that life as we know it should stop when a loved one dies is, I believe, one of these prototypical human experiences. Most humans have felt this way about witnessing the death of a loved one at some point. We have two primary ways to interpret the feeling: either it is a profound frustration caused by the absurdity of imposing meaning on an indifferent and meaningless world, or perhaps it is a reflection of the deeper reality that each human life is in truth just that significant. Perhaps the desire to "pour away the ocean and sweep away the wood" is not a coping mechanism or a flaw in our psychology, but rather an *acknowledgment* about the way things really are.

In death and suffering we experience the cross pressure between the closed, immanent frame's finality and our sense that love demands eternity. The kind of being a person is, their personhood, means they *ought* not have an end. And yet death comes for us all, and all around us we see its work in decay, violence, evil, sickness, and suffering. The weight of this cross pressure is too much for most of us to bear, so we have outsourced the burden of death to specialists: doctors, nurses, paramedics, law enforcement, fire departments, soldiers, and the like. We obsessively fight death, we push the sick and elderly to the margins of society, we quarantine the dying, we turn our fear of death into a quasicosmic war against global suffering. Yet, as Greene's character reminds us, "To be a human being one had to drink the cup." Here then is a cross pressure felt by all people at some point in their lives, and it has a clarifying power:

> Recognizing the tragedy in life is not just having the nerve to face it; it is acknowledging some of its depth and grandeur. There is depth, because suffering can make plain to us some of the meaning of life which we couldn't appreciate before, when it all seemed swimmingly benign; this is after all what tragedy as an art form explores. There is grandeur because of the way suffering is sometimes borne, or fought against. So in a curious way, a picture of life as potentially frictionless bliss robs us of something.[27]

Taylor's analysis of tragedy's clarifying effect suggests a way for Christians to bear a disruptive witness in a world that frantically works to deny and silence death.

167

When our neighbors suffer tragedy, we have an obligation to mourn with those who mourn (Romans 12:15). Entering into the mourning of others is an affirmation of the reality of loss, and it allows us to see more clearly what gives our lives meaning and value. The distractions of this age momentarily lose their attraction and the closed, immanent frame is revealed in stark contrast to our longing for eternity. But this clarifying vision is fleeting. Virtually every force in our culture militates against us contemplating our mortality and its implications. Rather than a traditional period of mourning as we find in other cultures and times, American culture encourages us to cope and move on.[28] We can offer a disruptive witness merely by weeping with those who weep, giving them space and dialogue to experience sorrow and to contemplate mortality, suffering, and evil. Our presence and openness to the weight of tragedy will itself be a witness to God's compassion and the significance of each human life. We don't have to explicitly share the gospel in these moments, though there will be times when it's appropriate to do so. We can bear witness by using language that comforts without trivializing death, suffering, and sorrow.

Our culture treats mourning as a mental health problem to be overcome. When something tragic occurs, we think in terms of its emotional/psychological consequences. As Christians, we should not mourn like those without hope (1 Thessalonians 4:13), but neither should we accept the therapeutic language of secular modernity. The loss of a human life is not just an *event* that causes a psychological *consequence*. The mourning we experience reflects the reality that each human life is significant and made in the image of God. Treating sorrow in this way affirms the pressure we feel toward a reality beyond the immanent frame, where the goodness and meaning are not absurdities but truths.

But while tragedy can help disrupt our distracted lives in a way that leads to growth and conviction, we can also turn it into yet another mask to give our lives weightiness. The heightened sense of existence that tragedy brings can be turned into a lifestyle choice, because in that suffering we feel truly alive. To have a disruptive witness, then, we must be careful not to fetishize suffering or turn it into an ideal. American poet and philosopher Ralph Waldo Emerson, writing about the death of his young son, explored our attraction to suffering and its ultimate inability to give us the existential validation we seek.

> There are moods in which we court suffering, in the hope that here, at least, we shall find reality, sharp peaks and edges of truth. But it turns out to be scene-painting and counterfeit. The only thing grief has taught me, is to know how shallow it is. That, like all the rest, plays about the surface, and never introduces me into the reality, for contact with which, we would even pay the costly price of sons and lovers.... I grieve that grief can teach me nothing, nor carry me one step into real nature.[29]

Why is it that some people go out of their way to get hurt, whether emotionally or physically? Why do some people intentionally harm themselves, get addicted, date abusive people, befriend untrustworthy people, obsess over failures, or listen to music to wallow in depression?[30] Emerson understood that sometimes when we "court" suffering we are looking for an experience of reality. We want to feel something deeply enough so that our existence, at least for a moment, matters. If we cannot discover validation through success and happiness, we might find it through suffering, to hurt deeply enough that we find the "sharp peaks and edges of truth."

The danger comes when we confuse the clarity that tragedy can bring with the existential validation that we can experience with tragedy. Notably, Emerson states that turning to suffering to find "real nature" is hopeless. In other words, the experience of suffering is not the thing itself. It does not make our lives more meaningful, valid, or real. As we mourn with those who mourn, it is not our job to determine if someone's suffering is *real* or a *lifestyle choice*, but we do have a responsibility not to turn suffering into a virtue or a higher form of spirituality. Ultimately, Emerson was wrong that grief could teach him nothing. Grief can awaken us to our mortality and to our longing for meaning that resonates in eternity, if we mourn with those who mourn.

CONCLUSION

The world reveals the Creator's majesty, the beauty of his goodness, and the goodness of being, and it calls us toward gratitude to him. Even in our distracted, secular age, these manifestations of God's goodness cannot be extinguished. But they can be rerouted, reframed, or retold as something glorious but mundane, having the appearance of transcendence but without its presence. A disruptive witness treats these manifestations of transcendence *as* manifestations of transcendence in the stories we tell and in the way we experience tragedy. Our calling is not to invent allusions to God in our lives but to reveal and affirm the ones that are already, necessarily there.

LARGE AND STARTLING FIGURES

The scariest thing about modern life is how comfortable most of us are even in our suffering and discontent—comfortable enough to be swept along in the flow without ever having to pause and consider how truly unbelievable it is to be alive. There are just enough notifications, just enough health choices to feel guilty about, just enough answers for why we matter, just enough nice things to keep us grudgingly satiated to prevent us from facing the human heart and the dread of being alone that resides there simmering beneath the electronic buzz of modern life. And it's the easiest thing in the world to make Christianity just one more identity waving at us for attention as we float along.

But it's not. The gospel is not a preference. It's not another piece of flair we add to our vest. It's something far more beautiful and disturbing. The gospel is the power to raise the dead, to proclaim the greatness of God in a fallen and confused world. To be a follower of Christ in the early twenty-first century requires a way of being in the world that resists being sucked into the numbing glare of undifferentiated preferences we choose from to define our identity.

The challenge facing us today is not so much the temptation to be relevant to the point that we lose the gospel, but the tendency to unknowingly accept a secular understanding of our faith while believing that we are boldly declaring the gospel. Virtually every institution in our society insists that we determine the shape of our lives by personally selecting from an ever-increasing set of patchwork ideologies. Regrettably, the Western church has often done a poor job of resisting this practice. The result has been that the church often sees itself as one worldview competing in the worldview marketplace, the rules and regulations of which are determined by the market, not their adherence to truth. Thus, we run the risk of not only damaging our witness to the watching world, but doing so without knowing it.

But the church does have the resources and practices needed to present a disruptive witness, if we will take the time and have the will to act. It begins by seeing more clearly the kind of marketplace of ideas that secularism and a distracted age have produced. When we understand how most modern discourse happens in a buffered space that inoculates all parties against deep change, and that we tend to move from discourse to discourse without time for reflection, we can begin to see how some practices in the modern church actually contribute to this problem by offering only a thin version of the faith in an antagonistic form. This Ichthus-eating-Darwin-fish strategy of Christian witness does nothing to reveal the depths of our sin or the grandeur of God's grace. Instead, it presents Christianity as just one more slogan or ideology among a million. Once we can see this, we can begin to look for better ways to communicate the incomprehensible reality of God's love.

The way we frame our faith, how we treat it as a subject, and when and where we choose to speak about it have a dramatic effect on our ability to go disrupt the buffered self. Within our conversations, making use of cultural works that evoke some of the hidden realities of life is one effective way to challenge someone to see the gospel afresh. Likewise, the beauty and tragedy of life and the natural world provides us important opportunities to work against the game of secularism and distractions, inviting us to dwell on truths that unsettle us and call for a satisfactory justification, which can only truly be found in God. The purpose of examining our interactions is to see how we treat the faith when we bear witness to it throughout our life.

Built into the traditional liturgy of the church are practices that counter the stultifying effects of the consumerist vision of belief. The Lord's Supper is the supreme act of disruptive witness, in stark contrast to the materialist world and the buffered self. It pulls against the way we think of ourselves as self-enclosed individuals by breaking into that self with a spiritual event grounded in history, occurring presently, with objective meaning. In addition to the spiritual disciplines and the sacraments, the liturgy of the church can create desire-forming habits that stretch our vision of reality beyond the immanent frame. All of these efforts require sacrifice on our part to go against the stream of culture and our own selfishness, but the consequences for ignoring these deep societal changes will be serious.

THE ALTERNATIVE

In the mid-twentieth century, most sociologists believed that we were in the midst of a process of secularization that would only continue, pushing religious belief to the margins of society.[1] Very few people would go to church, and even those who did would do so for vaguely secular reasons: to belong to a community, to feel some sense of purpose in life, to fulfill a sense of obligation to the past. But most people would see the absurdity and senselessness of believing in a God who cannot be quantified, tested, or observed.

The secularization theory, as it was called, was the sociological consensus in the mid-twentieth century, and not without cause. As our scientific knowledge improved and more of our illnesses could be cured, the spaces previously housed by God seemed to be filling up quite neatly. Nationally, America's values and morals were becoming more diverse and less grounded in Judeo-Christian teachings. Yet, despite all this solid reasoning and the near-consensus on the issue, here we are in 2018, still going to church, still adding new converts, and still a vibrant community. The secularization theory was wrong. Christianity remains popular in the United States, and the church is growing rapidly in the southern hemisphere. But while Americans haven't lost faith, the space that faith fills in our lives and our ability to effectively communicate what the Christian tradition means has changed.

Failure to reassess how we bear witness to our faith in the twenty-first century, and failure to take these societal changes into account, has had and will continue to have serious effects on the life of the church and our ability to have a prophetic voice in the world. The inertia of our society moves us away from thick beliefs in the transcendent toward thin beliefs in whatever we choose to shape our identity. The trends in evangelicalism reveal just how strong this inertia has been in the church, helping to produce megachurches that trade on emotive, self-help faith and passionate believers who find their identity in Christian sub-culture rather than Christ. If these trends continue, we can expect the church to dramatically weaken in the United States as Christianity as an identity becomes increasingly intolerable. It is easy to define part of our identity around Christianity when it gives us a sense of community and results in few conflicts, but socially accepted morals are changing, particularly on issues of sex, gender, and orientation.

Insofar as the church has bought into individual sovereignty and self-definition (think of how we talk about our "personal faith journey," for example), it will lack the thick resources and community necessary to respond to any other social movement based on these same principles. We have already begun to see this among many millennials who have grown up being taught by teachers, culture, parents, and even the church to be intently focused on defining their identity. How then, they wonder, can it be immoral for others to define their identity around different genders or orientations? If we accept expressive individualism, we will support traditional biblical sexual ethics only until they come in conflict with our identity, but no further. And when the social pressure to adopt more inclusive ethics increases, or when we discover an identity at odds with biblical norms, we will acquiesce.

In a culture where thin beliefs and continual distractions are the norm, the church will wither. By this I do not merely mean that traditional doctrines that have become socially unacceptable will be shed—although that may be the case—but also that the visions of the good life offered by other identities will be more attractive. For the beauty of the Christian faith to be visible, we cannot play by the rules of the game of secularism, which force us to the surface and shift our focus inward and away from commitment. The rules of this game are not well suited to reveal the truth of Christ because they assume that this is only a game, one in which we adopt certain roles according to our tastes and situation, while our true self always remains safely hidden, buffered from all outside forces. If we continue to play by these rules, the secularization theory of the 1960s still won't be correct, but a subtler secularism will pervade, weakening the church's witness and life.

THE ROAD TO A DISRUPTIVE WITNESS

Flannery O'Connor wrote that modern life poses a particular challenge for the "novelist with Christian concerns" because readers are less likely to share their beliefs: "When you have to assume that [the audience] does not [share your beliefs], then you have to make your vision apparent by shock—to the hard of hearing you shout, and for the almost-blind you draw large and startling figures."[2] I'd like to trouble this quote a bit by suggesting that in contemporary life, we are inundated with "large and startling figures." Everyone is shouting.

This isn't meant as a criticism of O'Connor, who was obviously speaking figuratively, but to point out that how we conceive of "shouting" and "startling figures" must adapt to our context. In a society awash with advertisements, arguments, viral videos, memes, satire, and violence, it is necessary to find the startling someplace else. Of course, if we try, we still can startle people by doing something outlandish like holding a rodeo in a church, bringing a lion on stage Sunday morning, or turning our church worship team into a rock band with lights and hair and high volume—but the congregation will only be startled in the same way they were when they watched a particularly funny Super Bowl ad. They will be impressed, but not disturbed from their life. To cause that, it takes something more—perhaps something much simpler—than these kinds of church spectacles. Consider, for example, the story told by Cormac McCarthy in his Pulitzer Prize–winning novel, *The Road*.

The postapocalyptic genre captivates the imagination of early twenty-first-century audiences, not only because of our deep anxieties about societal and natural order breaking down, but also because we are fascinated by a world without all of the sources of identity that structure our modern lives. McCarthy powerfully portrays this world in his novel. A reader of *The Road* may try to make the story about global warming or nuclear warfare, but McCarthy works against this by refusing to tell us what caused the end of civilization. Instead, he focuses his entire attention on the story of a father and his young son as they travel south to escape the relentless cold in a world that has lost all governments, security, and future. Cormac McCarthy's *The Road* is a beautiful example of a work of art that provides a disruptive witness to a world that has accepted secular ideas of belief and the self, and that keeps itself distracted to avoid questioning those beliefs.

What makes *The Road* such a potent example of disruptive witness is that McCarthy pulls away all the identities, beliefs, and distractions that tend to keep us from pausing and asking the difficult questions of life. Arguably, the most difficult and important question any human must answer is why not to commit suicide, and this question preoccupies McCarthy's story. His characters live in a dying, savage, and cruel world. At one point, a character tells the father that it is immoral to keep the son alive in such a world, because eventually he will be captured by cannibals, raped, and eaten. In this world, what could justify keeping a little boy alive? Why continue living if your own death and the torture of your son are inevitable? What makes this question so disturbing is not the violence inherent in it, but its implications for our own lives: once we get beyond all the structures and culture and values we've been raised with, underneath it all, do any of us really have a reason to continue living?

Surprisingly, McCarthy's characters answer this in the affirmative, and they do so in a way that offers a witness. They cling to the hope that by traveling south they will find the "good guys." Despite the fact that every single person they meet on the road is either dying or trying to kill them, the father and son have hope. Specifically, they have hope because the boy's goodness in the fallen world appears to the father as a sign of God's Word. Near the beginning of the novel, the nameless father remarks concerning his son, "If he is not the Word of God, God never spoke." In this remarkable novel, McCarthy unsettles our comfortable lives, forcing us to question what makes life meaningful and good, and provides a witness that transcends the immanent frame and materialist logic. Without divulging the ending, I will say that ultimately, goodness finds them, affirming their hope in the goodness of God, even in a world that feels profoundly godless.

It is this kind of witness that we are called to bear in the world today—a witness that defies secular expectation and explanation, that unsettles our neighbors from their technological/consumerist stupor, and that gambles everything on the existence and goodness of a transcendent (and immanent!) God, whose sacrificial love for us compels us to love in return.

ACKNOWLEDGMENTS

Despite the fact that my name appears on the cover of this book, its existence is owed largely to the influence, effort, and resources of others. I am grateful to my wife, Brittany, who gave me the time and space to write, supported me, and challenged my thinking. To my children, Nora, Quentin, and Frances, who tried to give me the time and space to write, who supported me and challenged my imagination and priorities. To my parents, who instilled in me a love of reading. To my dissertation advisor, Dr. Luke Ferretter, who introduced me to Charles Taylor's work and gave me the confidence to write. To Scott Cunningham, who modeled for me how to bear great burdens and still function as an academic. To Richard Clark, who brought me on to help found Christ and Pop Culture, giving me a platform and a voice. To Derek Rishmawy, who prayed for me. To all the readers and members of Christ and Pop Culture, who sharpened me, encouraged me, and inspired me over the last ten years. And to Francis Schaeffer, Ken Myers, Jamie Smith, and other Christian thinkers, whose words were there for me when I needed examples of intellectually vibrant Christianity. Without these people, this book would not exist.

NOTES

INTRODUCTION

[1]James K. A. Smith, *How (Not) to Be Secular* (Grand Rapids: Eerdmans, 2014), 140. See also Charles Taylor, *A Secular Age* (Cambridge, MA: Belknap Press, 2007), 37-45.

1 THE BARRIER OF ENDLESS DISTRACTION

[1]The following three paragraphs were adapted from a 2012 column and served as the inspiration for this book. See Alan Noble, "Penetrating the Electronic Buzz of the 21st Century for Evangelism," *Christ and Pop Culture* (blog), November 8, 2012, https://christandpopculture.com/citizenship-confusion-penetrating-the -electronic -buzz-of-the-21st-century-for-evangelism.

[2]Thomas de Zengotita, *Mediated: How the Media Shapes Your World and the Way You Live in It* (New York: Bloomsbury, 2005).

[3]These examples are my own. *Mediated* was written five years before the launch of Instagram.

[4]Emma Barnett, "Mindfulness: The Saddest Trend of 2015," *Telegraph*, January 8, 2015, www.telegraph.co.uk/women/womens-life/11331034/Mindfulness-the-saddest -trend-of-2015.html.

[5]One good place to start is Andy Crouch, *The Tech-Wise Family* (Grand Rapids: Baker, 2017).

[6]Daniel J. Levitin, *The Organized Mind: Thinking Straight in the Age of Information Overload* (New York: Penguin, 2015), 96-97.

[7]Ibid., 97-98.

[8]Ibid., 100.

[9]James K. A. Smith, *Desiring the Kingdom: Worship, Worldview, and Cultural Formation* (Grand Rapids: Baker Academic, 2009).

2 THE BARRIER OF THE BUFFERED SELF

[1]Charles Taylor, *A Secular Age* (Cambridge, MA: Belknap Press, 2007), 3.

[2]Ibid., 556.

[3]Ibid., 304.

[4]Ibid., 299.

[5]Ibid., 25.

[6]Ibid., 25-27.

[7]James K. A. Smith, *How (Not) to Be Secular* (Grand Rapids: Eerdmans, 2014), 48.

[8]Taylor's understanding of the move from a premodern world of shared faith to a modern world of endlessly contested faith naturally raises the question of whether the premodern world was the better world. There are no scales by which we could weigh the relative goodness of two massive epochs of Western civilization. How does one weigh liberty and human rights against order and community? Do the abuses of the medieval church outweigh the holistic vision of life it presented people? Do the scientific advances of modernity outweigh the dehumanization of technology? To my mind, the better question is, what can we do to mitigate the ills of modernity today? There is no returning to a premodern world, only a choosing to improve this one.

[9]I chose the example of uncritically supporting refugees, but my point here is not political at all. The example could just as well have been about someone uncritically adopting a radical antirefugee position.

[10]Charles Taylor, *The Ethics of Authenticity* (Cambridge, MA: Harvard University Press, 1991), 48.

[11]James K. A. Smith has done an excellent job identifying how incomplete this account of belief is. See his *Desiring the Kingdom* (Grand Rapids: Baker Academic, 2009), 63-71.

[12]Please note the qualifier "popular understanding of worldview." I recognize that there are diverse ways of conceptualizing and teaching worldview studies. That said, I do worry that worldview studies inherently drift toward reductionism and misapplication because it is by design an effort to categorize massive ideas.

[13]Taylor, *Secular Age*, 540.

[14]Taylor, *Ethics of Authenticity*, 23.

[15]Ibid., 542.

[16]Ibid., 543.

[17]Ibid., 489.

3 SEARCHING FOR VISIONS OF FULLNESS

[1]Charles Taylor, *A Secular Age* (Cambridge, MA: Belknap Press, 2007), 299.

[2]Ernest Becker, *The Denial of Death* (New York: Free Press Paperbacks, 1997), 50.

[3]Charles Taylor, *Sources of the Self* (Cambridge, MA: Harvard University Press, 1989), 42.

[4]See Annie Murphy Paul, "Personality Tests Are Popular, but Do They Capture the Real You?," NPR, June 25, 2016, www.npr.org/sections/health-shots/2016/06/25/483108905/personality-tests-are-popular-but-do-they-capture-the-real-you.

[5]John Calvin, *The Institutes of the Christian Religion*, trans. Henry Beveridge (Grand Rapids: Eerdmans, 1957), 37-38.

[6]Charles Taylor offers a mixed account of expressive individualism. Although he is one of the best philosophers at describing this phenomenon and its dangers, he does not think it is *necessarily* narcissistic or harmful: "The search for pure subjective expressive fulfillment may make life thin and insubstantial, may ultimately undercut itself. . . . But that by itself does nothing to show that subjective fulfillment is not good. It shows only that it needs to be part of a 'package,' to be sought within a life which is also aimed at other goods." Taylor, *Sources of the Self*, 511.

[7]Taylor, *Sources of the Self*, 507.

[8]Ibid., 51-52.

[9]Taylor, *Secular Age*, 299.

[10]"The self-glorification that he needed in his innermost nature he now looked for in the love partner. The love partner becomes the divine ideal within which to fulfill one's life. All spiritual and moral needs now become focused in one individual. Spirituality, which once referred to another dimension of things, is now brought down to this earth and given form in another individual human being." Becker, *Denial of Death*, 160.

[11]Ibid., 166.

[12]Taylor, *Secular Age*, 308.

4 DISRUPTIVE PERSONAL HABITS

[1] See the Time Well Spent website, timewellspent.io, and the article about the organization's cofounder Tristan Harris: Bianca Bosker, "The Binge Breaker," *Atlantic*, November 6, 2016, www.theatlantic.com/magazine/archive/2016/11/the-binge-breaker/501122.

[2] Matthew B. Crawford, *The World Beyond Your Head: On Becoming an Individual in an Age of Distraction* (New York: Farrar, Straus & Giroux, 2015), 11.

[3] Ibid., 252.

[4] David Foster Wallace, *This Is Water: Some Thoughts Delivered on a Significant Occasion, About Living a Compassionate Life* (New York: Little, Brown, 2009), 36.

[5] This deep belief has immediate economic ramifications. It's no coincidence that people who see themselves as the absolute center of the universe are the best consumers.

[6] The kind of knowledge I have in mind here is not factual but bodily. Think of the knowledge of your mother's love for you. That knowledge cannot be abstracted from the experience of being held and hugged by your mother as a child. For more on this idea, see James K. A. Smith, *Imagining the Kingdom* (Grand Rapids: Baker Academic, 2013), 31-73.

[7] See Alan Noble, "What I Learned About Lust and Beauty from a Flickr Voyeur," *Christ and Pop Culture* 2, no. 6 (2014), https://christandpopculture.com/learned-lust-beauty-flickr-voyeur.

[8] Calvin Seerveld, *Rainbows for the Fallen World* (Toronto: Tuppence Press, 2005), 49.

[9] Ibid., 23.

[10] One of the values of the double movement is that it reveals the inherently relational character of creation, which can help draw us out of the atomization of radical individualism.

[11] David Bentley Hart argues that modernity has created "narratives of the sublime." As philosophers reject the idea of Being as a presence, they replace it with an absence: "Being, no longer resplendent with truth, appearing in and elevating all things, could be figured then only as sublime." In this view, allusions always refer to other allusions endlessly, and there is no final thing or being to which to refer. David Bentley Hart, *The Beauty of the Infinite: The Aesthetics of Christian Truth* (Grand Rapids: Eerdmans, 2003), 44.

[12] Seerveld, *Rainbows for the Fallen World*, 52.

[13] Cormac McCarthy, *Blood Meridian* (New York: Vintage International, 1992), 124.

[14]Seerveld strongly condemns these kinds of kitschy paintings: "Kitsch oversimplifies emotional nuances and reduces aesthetically sensitive life to a one-track, predictable, pseudo-transcendent satisfaction." Seerveld, *Rainbows for the Fallen World*, 66. The gaudiness of kitsch draws attention to itself, but lacks the *allusiveness* to draw us out of our heads and up to God.

[15]Emmanuel Mounier, *Personalism* (Notre Dame, IN: Notre Dame Press, 2010), 18-19.

[16]Ibid., 19.

[17]Ibid., 20.

[18]Later in *Personalism*, Mounier writes: "Christian personalism goes the whole way, and deduces all values from the unique appeal of the one supreme Person," so it is possible that he would agree with my elaboration on his claim. Ibid., 68.

[19]Blaise Pascal, *Pensées*, trans. A. J. Krailsheimer (London: Penguin Books, 1995), 42-43.

[20]Ibid., 8.

[21]Ibid., 120.

[22]John Calvin, *The Institutes of the Christian Religion*, trans. Henry Beveridge (Grand Rapids: Eerdmans, 1957), 37-38; emphasis added.

[23]A word of caution: Not all guilt or anxiety has a discrete, identifiable source. Sometimes we just feel bad, or at least I do. In those cases, reflecting on these feelings can turn into an obsession—the kind of narcissistic focus that Mounier explicitly warns against. With time, prayer, and grace we can learn to discern false guilt and sourceless anxiety. Sometimes self-reflection ends in asking God to either bring revelation to a feeling or to help us bear the burden of it until it passes.

[24]Seerveld, *Rainbows for the Fallen World*, 62.

5 DISRUPTIVE CHURCH PRACTICES

[1]Charles Taylor, *A Secular Age* (Cambridge, MA: Belknap Press, 2007), 554.

[2]Ibid., 555.

[3]Ibid., 614.

[4]James K. A. Smith, *Desiring the Kingdom* (Grand Rapids: Baker Academic, 2009), 86.

[5]Ibid., 156.

[6]Ibid., 169.

[7]Ibid., 169.

[8]Ibid., 170.

[9]Ibid., 173.

[10]Ibid., 175.

[11]Taylor, *Secular Age*, 489.

[12]Smith, *Desiring the Kingdom*, 180.

[13]Ibid., 193.

[14]James K. A. Smith, *Imagining the Kingdom* (Grand Rapids: Baker Academic, 2013), 163.

[15]This distinction is important to make because emotions can be elusive. Some people appear to be more capable of having a mystical experience of God's presence than others. And some of us can run ourselves ragged overanalyzing whether an overwhelming feeling was God's conviction or just the result of a poor night's sleep. We should have grace for the way different people experience God. But what should not change is the *posture* and *tone* we convey about the *objective* reality of God's presence when two or more are gathered.

6 DISRUPTIVE CULTURAL PARTICIPATION

[1]Charles Taylor, *A Secular Age* (Cambridge, MA: Belknap Press, 2007), 309.

[2]Ibid., 595.

[3]Not all ways of shoring up faith in the face of cross pressures are healthy. Some may give us momentary shelter, but later leave us without hope. Presenting Christians in high school with a caricature of atheism and evolution will give them confidence up until the point they meet an actual atheist or enter a biology class.

[4]Taylor, *Secular Age*, 726.

[5]Ibid., 596.

[6]Ibid., 597.

[7]Ibid., 596.

[8]Ibid., 607.

[9]Ibid., 721.

[10]Ibid., 318.

[11]For an extensive, secular exploration of this phenomenon, see Ernest Becker, *The Denial of Death* (New York: Free Press, 1973).

[12]Taylor, *Secular Age*, 732.

[13]Ibid., 731.

[14]Ibid., 732.

[15]Ibid.

[16]Ibid., 360.

[17]Ibid., 555.

[18]C. S. Lewis, *Mere Christianity* (New York: Touchstone, 1996), 121.

[19]F. Scott Fitzgerald, *The Great Gatsby* (New York: Scribner, 2003), 117.

[20]Graham Greene, *The Heart of the Matter* (New York: Penguin Books, 2004), 112.

[21]Taylor, *Secular Age*, 720.

[22]Ibid.; emphasis mine.

[23]Ibid., 721.

[24]Agency is a defining feature of personhood (according to Mounier) and "ought" is a *moral* claim. Significantly, Taylor listed agency and morality as the two other points of cross-pressure, in addition to aesthetic sensibility. Taylor, *Secular Age*, 596.

[25]W. H. Auden, "Funeral Blues," *Selected Poems* (New York: Vintage International, 2007), 48-49.

[26]Peter Berger, *A Rumor of Angels: Modern Society and the Rediscovery of the Supernatural* (Garden City, NY: Anchor Books, 1970).

[27]Taylor, *Secular Age*, 318.

[28]There are notable exceptions to this. In communities that suffer from violence, it is not unusual to see family members wearing shirts that commemorate their lost loved ones. There is a lesson here: the denial of death is a kind of privilege.

[29]Ralph Waldo Emerson, "Experience," in *Essays* (Boston: Houghton, Mifflin, 1903), 48-49.

[30]Please note my emphasis on "some people." There are many different causes for things like addiction and self-harm, but it seems to me an inescapable truth that for *some* people, these choices are ways to feel alive.

CONCLUSION: LARGE AND STARTLING FIGURES

[1]See Peter Berger, *A Rumor of Angels* (Garden City, NY: Anchor Books, 1970), 16.

[2]Flannery O'Connor, "The Fiction Writer and His Country," in *Mystery and Manners: Occasional Prose*, ed. Sally Fitzgerald and Ryan Fitzgerald (New York: Farrar, Straus & Giroux, 1970), 34.